SIGNPOST

is a series that aims to reflect the views of the left and help create a common, progressive understanding of issues that matter.

SIGNPOST

will address a wide variety of subjects. Each publication in the series shall focus on a single topic that is significant in debates of the day, in a manner that is serious, informative, analytically sound and politically interventionist. The series will aim to bring advanced knowledge to the general readers and to activists in movements for social transformation.

SIGNPOST

is committed to analyses that are clearly written, attractively produced and moderately priced.

RIDING THE NUCLEAR TIGER

SIGNPOST ISSUES THAT MATTER

N. RAM

RIDING THE NUCLEAR TIGER

LeftWord

First published May 1999
by LeftWord Books
12 Rajendra Prasad Road
New Delhi 110 001
India

LeftWord Books *is a division of*
Naya Rasta Publishers Pvt. Ltd.
27–29 Bhai Vir Singh Marg
New Delhi 110 001
India

ISBN 81-87496-03-7 (hardback)
ISBN 81-87496-02-9 (paperback)

Typeset in Garamond, BankGothic and Frutiger

Printed at Progressive Printers
A 21 Jhilmil Industrial Area
Grand Trunk Road
Shahdara
Delhi 110 095
India

CONTENTS

PREFACE

Riding the Nuclear Tiger is an indictment of the Bharatiya Janata Party-led government's dangerous nuclear adventure. Meant for the interested layperson, it also seeks to answer experts, especially in the field of strategic studies. It presents a detailed critique of the official arguments in favour of the new policy and those of its supporters and apologists. It attempts an analysis of India's nuclear policy over the long term and of its two fundamental features, the pursuit of independence and a commitment to peace. It assesses the scientific and technological capabilities that the Indian nuclear programme has built over half a century. It tells the story of how the Hindu Right, in pursuing its longstanding chauvinist goals hijacked India's nuclear policy, with the active assistance of important sections of the nuclear energy and defence research establishments. Finally, it argues that it *is* possible for India to get off the tiger, if the basic principles that guided India's peace-oriented and independent policy are applied creatively to the new situation.

This tract is heavily indebted to T. Jayaraman, a theoretical elementary particle physicist who has written extensively on the scientific and technological aspects of India's weaponization programme and has, in his capacity as a scientist, demonstrated convincingly that

Pokhran-II and nuclear weaponization cannot be justified. At my request, he compiled a substantial body of scientific data, assessments and analysis for this work. This material is as important for the analysis as are the sections on policy and politics. Jayaraman's contributions would normally be recognized as that of a co-author. But he works at the Institute of Mathematical Sciences, Chennai, which although an autonomous institution, is funded, almost exclusively, by the Department of Atomic Energy; and, according to a bureaucratic interpretation of the conduct rules supposed to be in force, he is not allowed to express any critical assessment of 'any current or recent policy or action of the Government'.

This tract comes a year after the Pokhran-II explosions. One year is a sufficient time for the effects and implications of the benighted nuclear adventure to become clear to those who are willing to look at them without blinkers. What is also apparent is that nuclear weaponization in India and South Asia *is* reversible.

Nuclear weaponization can be undone in an achievable sequence of well-ordered steps which accept an order of priority that makes good sense. In India as elsewhere, there are several good democratic and progressive ideas about how this can be achieved. There are also some differences, notably on the CTBT, that can be treated as friendly differences, but must not be dodged in a democratic and progressive campaign against nuclear weaponization. Unilateralism had a progressive content in western Europe, as shown spiritedly in England up to 1983 by the Campaign for Nuclear Disarmament. But unilateralism in a context where imperialism is determined to force India into the discriminatory global nuclear order is *not* progressive.

Pre-Pokhran-II nuclear policy, with its balanced commitment to independence and peace, made excellent sense. This tract is a description and analysis of what went horribly wrong for the policy and why. But it also carries a message of hope by proposing an achievable agenda for de-weaponization, for getting off the nuclear tiger, without sacrificing either of the commitments on which the old policy was based. The agenda will continue to be relevant to policy and political practice through changes in regime – until, in fact, nuclear weaponization in India and South Asia is undone.

N. RAM

CTBT *Comprehensive Test Ban Treaty*

1

INTRODUCTION

The first significant act of the Bharatiya Janata Party (BJP)-led government after it came to power at the Centre in March 1998 was to hijack India's independent and peace-oriented nuclear policy and twist it out of shape. It was a policy that had been shaped over half a century of independence and withstood the test of various external challenges as well as pressures mounted by the enforcers of the Discriminatory Global Nuclear Bargain (DGNB). The essence of the bargain is the division of the world into five nuclear weapons states, the 'haves', and the rest, the 'have-nots', and the imposition of two completely different sets of rules for the two categories.

That the decision to explode five nuclear devices at Pokhran on May 11 and 13, 1998 and to weaponize the nuclear option was made pre-emptively, in the utmost secrecy, in the name of 'national security' – targeting especially China and Pakistan – and 'shakti', without any objective review or democratic discussion, in clear violation of the promises made in the National Agenda for Governance, in utter disregard of both the consequences for the region and the basic interests of the Indian people, was in keeping with the reactionary and authoritarian character of the decision. It was also in keeping with the character of the decision that within weeks the whole world could see the nuclear policy of the government of the Hindu Right swing from jingoistic adventurism to virtual capitulation to the terms laid down by the enforcers of the DGNB, principally the United States.

The early stance and statements of the government were nothing if not vainglorious. Within days of the Pokhran-II explosions, a high-placed expert formulated the Indian demand on the regime of the Nuclear Non-Proliferation Treaty (NPT) thus: 'Tell us what we are and we will tell you whether we can sign. Guarantee to us that technology controls, which you apply as though we were a non-nuclear weapons state, will be removed.'[1] In short, let us into the NPT regime as the sixth nuclear weapons state and we might play.

In the first official statement issued after the first round of Pokhran-II explosions, Brajesh Mishra, Principal Secretary to the Prime Minister, announced that 'India would be prepared to consider being an adherent of some of the undertakings in the Comprehensive Test Ban Treaty (CTBT)', adding: 'But this cannot obviously be done in a vacuum. It would necessarily be an evolutionary process from concept to commitment and would depend on a number of reciprocal activities.'[2] Soon after this, Prime Minister Atal Behari Vajpayee boasted in a magazine interview: 'India is now a nuclear weapon state. . . . [T]he tests . . . have given India shakti, they have given strength, they have given India self-confidence.'[3]

But it quickly became clear that the BJP and the Rashtriya Swayamsevak Sangh (RSS), the real command centre of the saffron brigade, had made an enormous miscalculation whose determining elements and assumptions bore no relation to contemporary international realities. This is why the effects and implications of Pokhran-II have been the opposite of what they were supposed to be, suggesting that the top decision-makers in the government failed in their minimum responsibility to think through the post-Pokhran-II scenario. Contrary to the triple boast of shakti, strength and self-confidence, the real achievement, it is now clear, has been to bring about India's near total isolation in the international arena and tremendously increase its vulnerability to strategic imperialist arm-twisting and pressure.

'Adventurism' describes the following specific steps: the government's pre-emptive action of conducting the nuclear explo-

DGNB *Discriminatory Global Nuclear Bargain*

sions, come what may; proclaiming India to be a nuclear weapons state, which had acquired the 'capacity to vacate' any nuclear threat to itself;[4] offering various confused ideas about India's new willingness to join, in some conditional way, the DGNB; making unfriendly statements against China and Pakistan; acting as though the high probability of Pakistan answering in kind never entered the policymaker's ken; and making a provocative linkage between the Kashmir issue and self-proclaimed nuclear weapons status.[5]

But the swing towards capitulation began immediately after Pokhran-II, with the government signalling the United States and its allies that India would now be willing to join the DGNB in some conditional way. In fact, the first inkling of the swing was provided by Mishra's May 11 statement offering to 'consider being an adherent to some of the undertakings in the Comprehensive Test Ban Treaty', even if he attached to this offer a rider that, in the light of what we now know about the policy swing, was meaningless. The stance that India would be able to impose conditions or terms on the discriminatory global nuclear order and win 'reciprocal' concessions as a *quid pro quo* for joining the CTBT was quickly abandoned without so much as an explanation.

Far from being able to assert any new-found 'shakti' in the international political arena, the Vajpayee government was forced to engage itself in a protracted, non-transparent negotiation with the United States over what India's nuclear weapons status can be allowed to be. It was clearly not a dialogue between equals. The government's claim was that it was involved in some delicate security-enhancing process of working out nuclear India's new place in the sun with its chief 'interlocutor', the United States. The reality is that the *interlocutor* has turned out to be an *intervenor*. For the first time in the history of India's nuclear policy, the United States is setting terms for, and shaping, the policy – driving it relentlessly towards signing and ratifying the profoundly inequitable CTBT, accepting previously rejected terms for the negotiation of a Fissile Material Cut-Off Treaty (FMCT), and making an unending series of other concessions in the strategic, foreign policy and economic spheres in order to get the economic sanctions lifted and India's *de facto* nuclear weapons status accepted. The adventure of conducting the nuclear explosions and rushing to declare India a full-fledged nuclear weapons state has turned out to be

CTBT *Comprehensive Test Ban Treaty*

an *akratic* misadventure, a sort of riding the tiger.[6]

EFFECTS OF THE NUCLEAR EXPLOSIONS

The removal of the element of self-restraint from India's nuclear policy and the unilateral, unprovoked conversion of the nuclear option as per a preset agenda were extremely harmful developments for the following reasons:

1. *Not surprisingly, the Pokhran nuclear explosions worsened regional tensions and already troubled relations with Pakistan.* Whatever rationalization the BJP and apologists of Indian nuclear weaponization might have resorted to, Chagai was understood by objective observers everywhere as the answer to the destabilizing Indian nuclear explosions: it is unlikely to have happened without Pokhran-II. With the eleven claimed explosions, South Asia became a much more dangerous place.

Pokhran-II and Chagai and the talk of weaponization, deterrents, deployment and use of nuclear weapons for 'self-defence' introduced a deadly new calculus in the Indo–Pakistan relationship. As part of the immediate political fallout from Pokhran-II but preceding the Chagai explosions of May 28 and 30, 1998 came statements from top persons associated with the government, notably Union Home Minister Lal Krishna Advani, that made them sound for a while like aspirant Unabombers. On both sides, scientists claimed that they had successfully contained the radioactive fallout, but the provocative linkage sought to be established between the Kashmir issue and self-proclaimed nuclear weapons status raised questions about the unstudied effects of distant radiation on the processes of human thinking. All this suggests that part of the calculation of the Hindu Right was the delusional belief, which manifested itself during the interregnum between Pokhran-II and Chagai, in an Indian strategic nuclear edge.

After the initial euphoria over the explosions wore out and competitive claims, boasts and putdowns about the two South Asian nuclear programmes generated much public confusion and anxiety, some conciliatory signals were sent out to Pakistan in an attempt to manage 'safely' what looked very much like a nuclear standoff. The resumption of the process of official dialogue at various levels, a process that must be welcomed and supported, led up to Prime Minister

Vajpayee's bus ride to the border and the Lahore summit. But, as we shall see later in this tract, what has come out of the Lahore exercise is far short of the minimum required to bring the situation back under control.

What is more, the test-firing of the extended range Agni II intermediate range ballistic missile (IRBM) on April 11, 1999, obliging a tit-for-tat response from Pakistan in the form of the test-firing of the Ghauri II missile on April 13, and the subsequent testing of the Shaheen and Trishul missiles by Pakistan and India respectively, introduced major new tensions in the Indo–Pakistan relationship. With Pakistan's government accusing the Indian government of aggravating the conventional imbalance and derailing the normalization process by introducing a 'new weapons system' in the region, and promising to maintain a 'reasonable deterrence in all areas, be it strategic or other weapons and indigenous missile programmes', it was clear that a risky and costly arms race was on, and the process of bilateral dialogue was under serious question if not in jeopardy.[7]

2. *Pokhran-II, and the run-up to it as well the follow-up, had an adverse and deplorable impact on Sino–Indian relations.* Before the explosions, Defence Minister George Fernandes in some public pronouncements signalled the BJP-led government's unfriendly attitude to socialist China. But it was Prime Minister Vajpayee's May 11, 1998 letter to U.S. President Bill Clinton that threatened to undermine Sino–Indian relations. The debris and dust had hardly settled at Pokhran when the following written message about 'the rationale for the tests' was on its way to the White House:

> I have been deeply concerned at the deteriorating security environment, especially the nuclear environment, faced by India for some years past. We have an overt nuclear weapons state on our borders, a state which committed armed aggression against India in 1962. Although our relations with that country have improved in the last decade or so, an atmosphere of distrust persists mainly due to the unresolved border problem. To add to that distrust that country has materially helped another neighbour of ours to become a covert nuclear weapons state. At the hands of this bitter neighbour we have suffered three aggressions in the last 50 years.[8]

This letter, which the Vajpayee government naively appears to have expected to remain confidential, revealed part of the motivation and game plan behind Pokhran-II. It provided an unmistakable early hint to U.S. imperialism that the government of the Hindu Right would be prepared to play along with the idea of a strategic anti-China alliance. In a magazine article written days after the Indian explosions, Aijaz Ahmad was among the first to call attention to this reactionary element in the game plan:

> This focus on China is deliberate, as the beginning of a methodical red-baiting offensive within the country, as the inauguration of an arms race on the Asian continent, and as an appeal to long-term U.S. goals in Asia. What we are witnessing is the staging of a short-term Indo–U.S. tension as a prelude to a long-term, comprehensive strategic alliance . . . the long-term prospect is for a closer anti-China axis between the U.S. and India. . . . Behind the BJP's bogus anti-imperialism and the American sanctions lies the prospect of a far-reaching alliance in a new Cold War.[9]

In the light of what has happened in the year after Pokhran-II, these observations must be recognized as prescient.

With the unfriendly statements preceding and following Pokhran-II, the heartening progress made since December 1988 in improving all-round relations with China was in danger of reversal.

Is it possible that we are making too much of the May 11, 1998 letter? Imagine a scenario in which Defence Minister Fernandes did not make his anti-China remarks and Prime Minister Vajpayee did not target China in his letter to Clinton by way of rationalizing the Pokhran-II nuclear explosions. Would China have reacted differently and would Sino–Indian relations have been in better shape? The answer to both questions is *yes*. The problematical implications of the nuclear explosions for Sino–Indian relations, and the effect of the political targeting of China in order to find a rationalization for the misadventure, are related but independent issues.

The author of this tract had the opportunity to visit China in August 1998 and test this hypothesis. He was able to explore, in some detail, the current state and future of Sino–Indian relations with Zhu Bangzao, official spokesman of the Chinese Ministry of Foreign Affairs, and several scholars specializing in the study of India, Sino–Indian relations and South Asia. Every one of them regretted the recent downturn in bilateral relations, identified the reasons for the setback, and set out clearly what needs to be done to bring the relationship back on track.

'I believe it is a wrong option for India to go nuclear', observed the official spokesman. But, he added,

> it is a greater mistake for India to accuse China and to use it as a pretext to conduct nuclear tests. In fact, on May 11, when India conducted its first tests, China exercised restraint in expressing its position. At quite a late point of time, we expressed our regret. I believe it was against the world trend, so we had to express our position. On May 13, after India conducted its second round of nuclear tests and the Prime Minister had sent a letter to President Clinton alleging that China posed a threat, China issued a statement of its Ministry of Foreign Affairs, which we haven't done for many years. . . . It was a strongly worded statement. Why? We didn't understand why India blamed China.

In the months following Pokhran-II, the BJP-led government did not make any overt move to further the reactionary project of the anti-China axis. It has attempted, in official level talks and informal exchanges at the political level, to repair the damage done to Sino–Indian relations by its statements and actions. Suggestions were made that External Affairs Minister Jaswant Singh should visit China to take up this repair work at a higher level. China's officially stated, perfectly justified position is that 'India must offer an explanation of what it has done. Secondly, Indian leaders should stop their accusations against China. Thirdly, the Indian Government should show its sincerity through deeds.'[10] Under these circumstances, progress has been slow.

India–China relations were under pressure again after the test firing of Agni II with Defence Minister Fernandes publicly claiming that 'we have reached a point where no one, anywhere, can threaten us' and talking about the capability of the IRBM system to carry nuclear warheads, and with some hawkish security analysts talking openly about 'a reliable nuclear delivery system to deter China', with a capability to 'reach Beijing and Shangai for sure'.[11]

3. *Pokhran-II and its follow-up have harmed India's reputation among peace-loving, democratic and progressive constituencies round the world.* Independent India's consistent policy over half a century was to advocate the abolition of nuclear weapons, seen from the start as being against 'the spirit of humanity'.[12] As early as 1948, India put forward a proposal at the United Nations for limiting the use of atomic

IRBM *intermediate range ballistic missile*

energy to peaceful purposes and eliminating nuclear weapons; two years later it called attention to the grave dangers of the nuclear arms race, highlighting in addition its character as a drain on human and economic resources that needed to be channelled into development. Jawaharlal Nehru and Krishna Menon emerged as leading world campaigners for the abolition of nuclear weapons without compromise, and India came up with a series of specific, practical proposals, including a genuine test ban, focussing on the imperative need for abolition.[13] The Six Nation Initiative launched by Indira Gandhi in 1983, the New Delhi Declaration by Rajiv Gandhi and Mikhail Gorbachev, and Rajiv Gandhi's 1988 Action Plan for a nuclear-weapons-free world order were important nuclear disarmament initiatives at the international level. A substantial part of Michael Foot's passionate and insightful book, *Dr Strangeglove, I Presume*, is an endorsement of these Indian initiatives and the opportunity they offered 'to achieve the biggest breakthrough ever in genuine world-wide disarmament', and an indictment of western government attitudes towards these initiatives.[14] 'The two key characteristics' of the Action Plan, an informed observer has pointed out in answer to tendentious post-Pokhran-II attempts to interpret the Rajiv Gandhi initiative in the service of the weaponization-and-CTBT-joining cause, are that 'it establishes a defined time-frame within which the objective of nuclear weapons elimination is to be achieved' and 'sets out the identifiable, verifiable phases through which the goal of elimination is to be achieved'.[15]

With their nuclear misadventure, the government of the Hindu Right and the strategic affairs apologists have attempted to lay a rich fifty-year legacy to waste, and in doing so have alienated people of goodwill everywhere.

4. *While the U.S.-led economic sanctions, based on unacceptable double standards, against India must be condemned and opposed, the BJP-led government must take full responsibility for the additional pressure that imperialism has brought to bear on the Indian economy after Pokhran-II.* Immediately after the nuclear explosions, a contradiction seemed to be developing between the government's 'soft' pro-liberalization economic policy and its 'hard-line' hawkish nuclear and security stance. It turned out to be no real contradiction at all: even as nuclear adventurism swung quickly towards compromise with,

CTBT *Comprehensive Test Ban Treaty*

or capitulation to, the discriminatory global nuclear order, the government felt pressured to come up with a policy of economic appeasement.

The RSS-sponsored propaganda line that the economic sanctions imposed by the United States and some of its allies would not make much of a difference to a huge continental economy such as India's began to wear thin within weeks of the imposition of sanctions. The economist Jayati Ghosh, writing in June 1998, accurately predicted the real effects of economic sanctions.[16] There was little doubt that Pakistan's 'very fragile' economy would be hit harder by sanctions. It was also apparent that the direct effect of sanctions for India would be chiefly in terms of reduced bilateral aid, reduced multilateral financing and, more substantially, the closure of credit lines for companies dealing with or in India. Nevertheless 'it is definitely not the case that these sanctions will not affect the economy much, or that their impact will be limited to the specific areas in which they have been imposed'. The real effect of sanctions, she predicted, would be 'much broader and more painful, if they succeed in reducing international investor confidence in a government that is desperate to attract foreign investment'. Some months later, Strobe Talbott, U.S. Deputy Secretary of State, would publicly advise India that a decline in the flow of foreign capital was 'perhaps the most serious economic threat'.[17]

The proof of the sanctions-immune Indian economy and the sanctions-defying official Indian stance can be seen in the actual response in both economic and political areas. The government of the Hindu Right certainly behaved as though the country could not bear the reality of prolonged economic sanctions, especially when the economy was in serious difficulty. Meanwhile, the United States, adopting a carrot-and-stick approach, was able to play upon official Indian fears and apprehensions *vis-à-vis* the severity and duration of sanctions and soften up the policy response further.

It is becoming increasingly clear to Indian policy-makers that actual nuclear weaponization will not come cheap. Some quick estimates by economists suggest a ballpark range of Rs 40,000 crores to Rs 50,000 crores as the minimum cost of a nuclear weaponization programme, defined as 'acquiring a second strike capability comprising a triad delivery (that is, by aircraft, land-based missiles and submarines) of 150 bombs', over the next decade, which works out to Rs 4000 crores to Rs 5000 crores a year.[18] These economists point out that this will be the additional burden coming on top of conventional defence expenditure; and also that escalation tends to be built into nuclear weaponization programmes since an arms race is guaranteed. Such estimates must be very worrying to the Finance Ministry and to economic policy-makers. Further, this kind of profligate spending in the name of nuclear defence means an unconscionable diversion of public resources from what needs urgently to be spent on the social sector and development.

Finally, there is another big cost, which Jayati Ghosh characterizes as 'the most important economic cost' of the Pokhran-II misadventure.[19] This is a period when the countries and institutions of the Washington Consensus have been imposing sovereignty-eroding policies on the less developed countries. These policies force vulnerable economies to restructure in such a way that enormous new burdens are imposed on the masses of the people and doors are opened wider and wider to foreign capital. The appeasement policies followed by the BJP-led government after the nuclear explosions have enabled the enforcers of the Washington Consensus, led by the United States, to tighten their grip over India's economic and political policies in a manner that could not have been foreseen in, say, early 1998.

5. *India is weaker and much more vulnerable to external pressure and arm-twisting than it was pre-Pokhran-II and pre-Chagai and U.S. imperialism, seeking to impose its strategic hegemony on the region, has emerged as the arbiter of the Indo–Pakistan nuclear standoff and as the intervenor shaping the future of India's nuclear policy.* On Day One, when Vajpayee wrote to Clinton blaming China for Pokhran-II, 'the ball was set rolling for the United States to dictate terms to India'.[20] Interestingly, in its calibration of sanctions against India and Pakistan, the United States has decided to resume the International Military Education and Training Programme (IMET) for India while keeping in place sanctions targeted at India's economic and technological development. The expert-level Indo–U.S. talks designed to see that India tightened its export control regime were an example of the extent to which the BJP-led government was prepared to go to appease the United States. Kashmir and other outstanding issues between India and Pakistan have figured in the parallel Indo–U.S.

and Pakistan–U.S. dialogue, and the resumption of the Indo–Pakistan dialogue on a wide range of issues, including Kashmir, seems, at least in part, the result of U.S. pressure on an increasingly vulnerable Indian government. The BJP-led government's conspicuous failure to come up with a forthright condemnation of the recent military aggression by the United States and the United Kingdom against Iraq and of the bombing of Yugoslavia by forces of the North Atlantic Treaty Organization (NATO) headed by U.S. imperialism also testified to an official Indian policy that lacked backbone.

6. *Last and most important of all, the government of the Hindu Right has exposed the people of India and Pakistan to the infinite horrors that nuclear weapons can inflict.* This will become clear as the argument in this tract proceeds.

THE POLITICAL RESPONSE

After the early euphoria wore out and some of the harmful effects became evident, there was deepening political and intellectual opposition to the BJP-led government's nuclear adventurism. A number of political parties, including the Congress (I), joined the Left parties which, from the beginning, took a firm stand against Pokhran-II and nuclear weaponization. A broad-based campaign against nuclear weapons with a coherent agenda opposing both nuclear adventurism and the policy swing towards capitulation to the DGNB took shape and protest meetings, rallies and conventions were organized in various centres round the country (see box overleaf).

In the parliamentary debate that followed the nuclear explosions, the Opposition drawn from the Left parties, the Congress (I), the Janata Dal and some other parties clearly had the better of the exchange. The Vajpayee government found itself very much on the defensive. Aside from representatives of the Communist Party of India (Marxist) and the Communist Party of India, former Prime Ministers H.D. Deve Gowda, Chandra Shekhar and Inder Kumar Gujral, former Finance Ministers Manmohan Singh, P. Chidambaram and Pranab Mukherjee, and former Minister of State for External Affairs K. Natwar Singh effectively challenged the government's decision to remove the element of conditional self-restraint from India's nuclear policy and to weaponize. They highlighted the dangerous escalation of tensions in the region, the harmful diversion of national resources

DGNB *Discriminatory Global Nuclear Bargain*

to a nuclear arms race, and the break with long-standing Indian nuclear policy. Many speakers criticized the jingoism and militarism that had been inducted into India's foreign policy, particularly in relation to China and Pakistan.

In the campaign for the November 1998 Assembly elections, which dealt severe blows to the BJP's prospects of stabilizing its rule at the Centre, Congress (I) president Sonia Gandhi is reported to have attacked the Vajpayee government's nuclear policy on several counts: for failing to prevent India's international isolation, for providing the opportunity for 'everybody outside India to talk about our internal problems', including Kashmir, for mishandling relations in the region, and for displaying a wrong sense of priorities.[21] The saffron debacle in Rajasthan, Delhi and Madhya Pradesh proved beyond any doubt that the masses of the people, alienated by sharp rises in the prices of essential commodities and by the manifestly communal, divisive and inept performance of the government of the Hindu Right, were not willing to buy the pseudo-nationalist and chauvinist agenda based on nuclear hawkishness, efforts to saffronize education, and minority-baiting.

A SPIRITED AND EFFECTIVE CAMPAIGN

If the BJP-led government had imagined that it would be able to hijack India's nuclear policy and open the floodgates of jingoism without significant resistance, it was quickly disabused of such ideas.

Within a few days of the Pokhran-II nuclear explosions, a surge of criticism began to be directed at the Government, questioning the timing, the motivation and the wisdom of conducting the tests. Among the political parties, the sharpest reactions came from the Left. In a jointbstatement, the Left parties condemned the tests and drew attention to the dangers posed to the peoples of the sub-continent if nuclear weaponization were to proceed. Opposing any attempt to sign the CTBT, this position upheld the imperative need to persist with a peace-oriented, independent nuclear policy. The rationale for conducting the Pokhran-II nuclear explosions was questioned also by other opposition parties, particularly after Vajpayee's letter of May 11 to Clinton became public knowledge.

Significant popular protests also began to be organized across the country. In Delhi and Mumbai, there were demonstrations involving public figures, journalists, trade unionists, workers, activists of the democratic women's movement, popular science activists, academics and other sections of society. By the beginning of June 1998, the campaign against nuclear weapons in the sub-continent began to take off. Conventions against nuclear weaponization were organized in several cities and towns round the country. The June 9 convention in Delhi, one of the first

CTBT *Comprehensive Test Ban Treaty*

to be organized, witnessed the participation of the general secretaries of the two Communist Parties, trade union leaders, activists of the popular science movement, public figures and academics. Among its highlights was the participation of Admiral L. Ramdas, former Chief of the Naval Staff, who, with his distinguished experience in the defence establishment, has become one of the most authoritative critics and opponents of the policy of nuclear weaponization in South Asia.

Other important conventions followed in Thiruvananthapuram, Calcutta, Mumbai and Chennai. The Chennai convention was notable for its mass mobilization and range of speakers and participants. It attracted professionals, leading scientists from various disciplines, including nuclear science, social and political activists, workers, journalists, social scientists, and trade union and political leaders. The participation in the convention of the writer, Arundhati Roy, who read from her powerful and passionate essay against nuclear weapons, 'The End of Imagination', became a major media event. The participation of Dr M.S. Swaminathan, the eminent agricultural scientist and geneticist, was another highlight. Aside from such conventions, meetings, discussions, rallies and exhibitions on the horrors of nuclear war were organized across the country.

Another significant early intervention in the debate was a statement signed by a large group of Indian scientists, drawn mostly from the younger generation (working both at home and abroad), that condemned the tests and warned the people about the dangerous implications of nuclear weapons from a scientific angle. Among other things, this intervention put paid to the official propaganda that the nuclear tests were a great and glorious achievement of Indian science. It drew fresh attention to the horror of nuclear war and the implications of a nuclear arms race in South Asia.

A high point in the Indian campaign against nuclear weapons was reached in the mass observance of Hiroshima and Nagasaki Day across the country on August 6 and August 9. Calcutta led the way with a large number of processions that crisscrossed the metropolis throughout the day on August 6; the total participation was estimated at 400, 000. This was, in all likelihood, the world's largest Hiroshima Day protest in 1998. The mass protest was the culmination of a well-prepared campaign that began with a unique resolution adopted by the West Bengal Assembly condemning the Pokhran-II tests and the BJP government's nuclear weaponization policy and calling for a mass protest on Hiroshima Day. The Delhi demonstrations were distinguished by the participation of a number of public figures constituting virtually a who's who of democratic and secular personalities in Indian public life. Spirited protests were staged in other parts of the country, extending in some States beyond the major metropolitan centres to district centres and small towns.

The democratic campaign against nuclear weaponization needs to press on with a principled stand on the issues it has identified as vital to the challenge of achieving de-weaponization; this means exerting constant pressure on Indian nuclear policy for now and the conceivable future, regardless of who is in government in New Delhi. Aside from participating in mass campaigns that take the message of the dangers of nuclear weapons to the people in every part of the country, the campaign must develop a detailed knowledge and information base that can help defeat the reactionary line of abandoning the two basic tenets of longstanding Indian nuclear policy – the peace orientation and the pursuit of independence.

However, the Rajya Sabha debate of December 1998 revealed that the democratic campaign against nuclear weaponization had much work to do if the hope was to see India's nuclear policy return to a sound peace-oriented and independent track once the BJP-led government fell and a successor government took over. The most significant feature of the substantive debate was that Congress (I) speakers, notably Pranab Mukherjee, failed to differentiate themselves from the Vajpayee government's nuclear policy approach. The senior Congress (I) leader appeared to accept Vajpayee's premise that nuclear weaponization in South Asia was a *fait accompli*, while maintaining a non-committal and non-oppositional stance on the CTBT.[22]

If Pranab Mukherjee's compromising articulation of his party's stand on these issues could be taken to reflect the emerging Congress (I) position, the main opposition party appeared to be preparing for a role when it would have to handle nuclear policy and these tricky issues in government. On the other hand, the fact that oppositional voices, such as Mani Shankar Aiyar's, Natwar Singh's and Madhya Pradesh Chief Minister Digvijay Singh's, within the Congress (I) on Pokhran-II continue to be active suggests that a final decision on which way India's nuclear policy will go under a Congress (I)-led dispensation is yet to be taken and can be influenced by a clear-sighted and effective democratic campaign.

EXPLAINING THE MISADVENTURE

Was the BJP-led government motivated to undertake its nuclear adventure by any anti-imperialist aim of challenging the unequal and discriminatory global nuclear order? Can it be given any kind of benefit of doubt in this regard? The answer is 'No'. As Prakash Karat points out in an analysis of the link between Pokhran-II and the BJP–RSS agenda, 'the BJP has not been motivated by any anti-imperialist aims to challenge the existing nuclear order. It is essential to differentiate between anti-imperialism and jingoism. The build-up and rationale for the Pokhran tests was the security threat posed by China

CTBT *Comprehensive Test Ban Treaty*

and its support to Pakistan. This was an obvious pitch to neutralize opposition from the United States'.[23]

The cynical subversion of India's long-standing policy opposition to the DGNB held in place chiefly by U.S. imperialism was evidenced by the following revelation made by the journalist and BJP Member of Parliament, Arun Shourie, in the Rajya Sabha debate on December 15, 1998. Shourie quoted Minister of External Affairs Jaswant Singh as explaining to him, in the manner of a schoolmaster to a favourite pupil, what had happened to India's nuclear policy with Pokhran-II: 'Look at it as a crowded railway compartment. When you are trying to come into it, your perspective is one. When you are in it, you want the rules that will keep you in and keep the others out'.[24]

Various explanations have been proposed in the media (by the government's spokespersons, by strategic affairs analysts, and by plain apologists) for why the Vajpayee government undertook the nuclear explosions and weaponization. The two most common explanations offered during the initial phase of euphoria sought to present Pokhran-II as a logical culmination of India's nuclear energy programme and policy and as an unstoppable achievement of India's scientific-technological capabilities. In a detailed statement made in Parliament within two weeks of the explosions, Prime Minister Vajpayee sought to make these explanations official by claiming that Pokhran-II was 'a continuation of the policies' that put India on the path of self-reliance and independence of thought and action, and that nuclear weapons status was 'an endowment to the nation by our scientists and engineers'.[25] These explanations either miss or deliberately cover up the link, well-acknowledged in RSS circles, between the government's decision to acquire nuclear weapons and the Hindutva agenda of the BJP and, ultimately, of the RSS.

Giving nuclear teeth to a Hindu Rashtra has been part of the ideology and programme of the RSS from the 1950s. Prakash Karat offers the following insight:

> The RSS has long dreamt of making India a chauvinistic–militaristic power based on majoritarian rule. For such a Hindu Rashtra to succeed, it must be able to mobilize people around an aggressive anti-Muslim platform and to create a permanent divide between Hindus and Muslims that can justify an authoritarian state. That is why in the

DGNB *Discriminatory Global Nuclear Bargain*

> 1960s, when India achieved nuclear capability, the Bharatiya Jan Sangh became a fervent advocate of making the bomb. The bomb was the mascot of the RSS long before the Ram temple acquired religious-political overtones for it in the 1980s. If the BJP's climb to power was aided by the temple-mosque controversy at Ayodhya, with the party coming to power at the Centre, the RSS has set out the next step in its long-term agenda of India making the bomb. The consequent escalation of tensions between India and Pakistan is part of the agenda. Viewed in this light, the retaliatory tests undertaken by Pakistan are what the RSS–BJP hoped would happen. Hence, to see the Pokhran tests as a natural culmination of India's nuclear policy from the 1950s is not only naïve but harmful to the very basis of a secular democratic Indian state.[26]

The anti-China motivation was equally evident. Hindu Rashtra ideology has traditionally seen China, along with Pakistan, in hostile and fanciful terms. The project of giving nuclear teeth to a Hindu Rashtra is related to such threat perceptions. In 1965, RSS supremo 'Guruji' M.S. Golwalkar characterized socialist China as 'the one common menace to entire humanity' and looked forward to a superpower and global alliance to destroy it.[27] 'The possession of [the] atom bomb by Communist China', he advocated, 'has made it imperative for us to manufacture the same. That alone will ensure confidence in the minds of the people and the armed forces about our ability to achieve ultimate victory. No doctrinaire or academic inhibitions should be allowed to come in the way.'[28]

What is clear from this is that the Vajpayee government, for all the limitations placed on the BJP's agenda by its coalition partners, launched its nuclear adventure in a preconditioned, pre-programmed way. Given the agenda and mindset, it followed as a matter of strategic political necessity that no one within the government could be asked to carry out any kind of objective or professional appraisal of the policy requirements, that no one could be given a chance to question or criticize the pre-empted course and the assumptions and motivations behind it. Indeed, it turns out from the public testimony of the scientists at the New Delhi press conference of May 17, 1998 that the go-ahead for the Pokhran explosions was given on or around April 12, 1998 – that is, within a month of the communal government's taking office.[29]

It is noteworthy that while the BJP did not include its demands on Ayodhya, Article 370 and a Uniform Civil Code in the National Agenda For Governance, it brought on board, without any fuss or resistance from its coalition partners, its well-known nuclear and security policy hawkishness. This must be seen in linkage with the anti-China predilections of influential coalition partners, notably Defence Minister George Fernandes, and the tension-raising policies virtually guaranteed by such a dispensation *vis-à-vis* Pakistan.

The National Agenda For Governance promised the following sequence of steps: the establishment of a National Security Council (NSC) 'to analyse the military, economic and political threats to the nation, also to continuously advise the government'; the undertaking of 'India's first ever Strategic Defence Review' by the NSC; a re-evaluation of nuclear policy; and, presumably if warranted by the NSC's Strategic Defence Review and re-evaluation of nuclear policy, the 'exercise' of 'the option to induct nuclear weapons'.[30] The suggestion of a review or re-evaluation was a smokescreen for a decision already made by the RSS–BJP top leadership. (This skipping of the promised sequence may have helped as much as anything else to fool the U.S. intelligence agencies.)

We now know from the joint general secretary of the RSS, K.S. Sudarshan, as well as from other sources, that there was a plan to go in for nuclear explosions and weaponization when Vajpayee formed the government in 1996. But since that government collapsed within thirteen days, the plan could not be put into effect.[31]

In contrast to government spokespersons and strategic affairs apologists, the RSS has made no bones about the fact that its agenda was the inspiration for the Vajpayee government's nuclear adventure. The May 17, 1998 issue of *Organiser*, thinly disguised as a Pokhran-I anniversary special, was actually released in advance to coincide with Pokhran-II.[32] The collection of hawkish and virulently anti-China and anti-Pakistan articles reiterated the well-worn RSS line that the bomb had to be made to 'tame Pakistan' and teach China a lesson for occupying Indian territory. One report in the issue quotes the RSS supremo or Sarsanghchalak, Rajendra Singh, 'himself a noted nuclear physicist', as expressing the following view:

> 'Pokhran has sent an important message to the world.' . . . The long-drawn cold war between the U.S. and the USSR had rendered conventional warfare redundant, he points out [*sic*] and attributes the

> military ambition of the West to their advance in nuclear research. In India we have always maintained that knowledge is for universal welfare (*sarvabhootahite ratah*) and not for destruction, says the Sarsanghchalak. But it does not mean that we should pay less attention to defence preparedness. We cannot afford to forgo our nuclear option when everyone around is arming himself to the teeth. Nuclear arsenal [*sic*] is an effective deterrent, he says [*sic*] and convincingly pleads that in the long run, a nuclear weapon is more economical than a huge stockpile of Sukoi craft and Bofors guns.[33]

THE CASE FOR THE DEFENCE

The defence put up by the BJP and other supporters and apologists of Pokhran-II, nuclear weaponization, and the policy swing towards joining the CTBT, the FMCT and the discriminatory global nuclear order, may be summarized as follows:

The necessity arose out of a changed security situation dominated by threats from neighbouring countries, above all China and Pakistan, and national security was 'the touchstone that has guided us in making the correct choice'.

Nuclear weapons are instruments of deterrence and therefore of peace. The objective of the new policy put in place by the Vajpayee government is not to engage in a nuclear arms race, but to establish a new equation and equilibrium in the region and in the world – through the development of a 'minimum credible nuclear deterrent', including a second-strike capability, and the offer of no first-strike and other 'confidence building measures'.

India's nuclear policy vision extends beyond South Asia. The possession and deployment of nuclear weapons, within the parameters indicated above, enhance India's status and role in international politics.

Pokhran-II represents something of a peak in scientific and technological accomplishment, a vindication of the efforts of two or more generations of Indian scientists, an unstoppable achievement of Indian science.

It represents a continuation and crowning of the country's long-term nuclear policy.

The basic justification for abandoning the earlier opposition to the CTBT and the FMCT is that India, having exploded its way to the status of a 'have', has no hang-ups (political objections or ethical constraints) in joining the DGNB. The primary and only material objection to the CTBT (and the FMCT under negotiation) was the consideration of national security, and Pokhran-II and the follow-up have taken care of

CTBT *Comprehensive Test Ban Treaty* FMCT *Fissile Material Cut-Off Treaty*

that. Once inside the 'crowded railway compartment', India is happy to support 'the rules that will keep you in and keep the others out'.

This tract will attempt to demonstrate that every one of these arguments is without foundation.

Chapter 2 deals with the nature of nuclear weapons and the horror – and unwinnability – of nuclear war. It also briefly considers the economic cost of nuclearization. Chapter 3 examines the theory of nuclear deterrence – with its essential features and the fallacy that deterrence is a guarantee against holocaust. Chapter 4 contests the claim of continuity between five decades of national consensus on nuclear policy in India and the benighted policy imposed on the people of India by the government of the Hindu Right. Chapter 5 has three parts: it challenges the idea that Pokhran-II is, in scientific terms, a great and glorious achievement; it reviews the proactive, often hawkish and weapons-friendly role that certain senior scientists in the nuclear establishment have played; and it assesses the claim that India is now a nuclear weapons state. Chapter 6 deals with the question of whether nuclear weapons can enhance national security in South Asia. Chapter 7 looks at the swing of the BJP-led government's nuclear policy towards capitulation in respect of the CTBT and the FMCT-to-come. It does this against the background of the well-articulated objections made in the past to joining these corollaries of the NPT. Chapter 8 is a concluding chapter in which we summarize our arguments and discuss the prospects for a reversal of post-Pokhran-II nuclear policy and the circumstances in which such a reversal can become reality. It proposes a five-point democratic and progressive agenda for de-weaponization in India and Pakistan.

DGNB *Discriminatory Global Nuclear Bargain* **NPT** *Nuclear Non-Proliferation Treaty*

2

THE HORROR OF NUCLEAR WEAPONS

A reasonable question arises about the Pokhran explosions of May 1998 and nuclear weaponization even among those who are opposed to the BJP–RSS agenda and do not consider themselves nuclear hawks. If five member-states of the United Nations – the United States, Russia, the United Kingdom, France and China – can be recognized as legitimate 'nuclear weapons states' by the NPT regime, allowed to function as an exclusive 'nuclear weapons club', and permitted to retain and do with their nuclear arsenals as they please, without making any concrete commitment to nuclear disarmament within a stipulated time frame, why should India not acquire nuclear weapons? Or to put it more fairly and objectively, why should not both India and Pakistan acquire nuclear weapons in a profoundly asymmetrical and unequal world?

In order not to underestimate the significance of this question, let us set out in some detail the prima-facie case for answering it in the affirmative.

Arms limitation and reduction agreements, as well as some unilateral national decisions and developments, have brought about significant changes in the size of nuclear arsenals and shifts in where the nuclear weapons and warheads are stored and deployed. This

NPT *Nuclear Non-Proliferation Treaty*

'downsizing' and these shifts are largely the result of the pressure mounted by the spirited struggles conducted by the people in various, notably western, countries, in the 1960s, 1970s and 1980s against the nuclear arms spiral and for universal nuclear disarmament. Some experts hold out hope for further significant downsizing in the intermediate future as a consequence of projected reductions by the United States and Russia under Strategic Arms Reduction (START) treaties. It is also pointed out that with the cessation of nuclear explosive testing, the development of new nuclear warheads will be slowed down.[1]

Nevertheless, what remains of the nuclear arsenals is of monster proportions, more than sufficient to destroy the world many times over. Whereas the total stock of nuclear warheads in the arsenals of the five nuclear weapons states as late as 1993 was reliably estimated to be in excess of 50,000, expert appraisals made at the end of 1997 put the total number at a still huge 36,000.[2] These weapons were stored at some 142 locations worldwide: U.S. nuclear weapons at 24 locations in 14 states and seven European countries; Russian nuclear weapons at some 90 locations, all in Russia; British nuclear weapons at two locations; French nuclear weapons at four locations; and Chinese nuclear weapons at some 20 locations.

The stark fact is that the nuclear weapons states have consistently refused to commit themselves, let alone to disarmament here and now, even to a time-bound process of negotiations for the abolition of nuclear weapons. They have ruled out any linkage between time-bound disarmament and the imposition of NPT corollaries, such as the CTBT and the FMCT, on states that are not 'permitted' to possess nuclear weapons. Not surprisingly, U.S. imperialism is the most zealous and uncompromising defender of its 'right', under the NPT regime, to keep a mighty nuclear arsenal in shipshape, state-of-the-art order and to invest in 'a modernized, lean-and-mean, nuclear armed future'.[3]

Since the United States cannot hope ever to regain its monopoly over nuclear weapons, it seeks the next best thing for itself – strategic military superiority that is premissed, above all, on a combination of advanced nuclear weaponry and anti-ballistic missile systems as soon as feasible. It is the arrogant pursuit of world dominance and strategic military superiority that rules out the possibility of even a paper commitment by the United States to 'no-first-use' of nuclear weap-

CTBT *Comprehensive Test Ban Treaty* FMCT *Fissile Material Cut-Off Treaty*

ons and 'no-use' of nuclear weapons against non-nuclear weapons states. It bears recall that during the 1991 Gulf War against Iraq, the United States and its leading allies pointedly refused to rule out in advance the use of nuclear weapons.

President Clinton's statement on Thanksgiving Day 1997 ('In this new world, our children are growing up free from the shadows of the Cold War and the threat of nuclear holocaust') was given the lie within days by news that U.S. plans for fighting a nuclear war had been revised by a Presidential Decision Directive (PDD). This was a 'disturbing' reminder that 'the United States still had plans for nuclear war'. The 'new modest changes', according to Robert Bell, a member of the U.S. National Security Council, were that the PDD was to be implemented with a maximum of about 8000 strategic warheads; that the PDD list of targets in China had been expanded; and that a few new countries had been added to the list.[4]

But it is not merely the United States that insists on continuing the division of the world into nuclear weapon 'haves' and 'have-nots'. It is true that 'treaty reductions, technological obsolescence, a lack of finances, and new concerns about physical security as a result of the break up of the Soviet Union' have taken a significant toll of the Russian nuclear arsenal.[5] While being at a significantly lower level than the mighty arsenal of the Soviet Union in its heyday, the current Russian stockpile of over 22,500 nuclear weapons, of which 10,240 are regarded as operational, is still a nuclear arsenal of disturbing proportions. Further, Russia continues nuclear warhead production on a significant scale; has several thousands of warheads on reserve[6] ; ratification of START-II has been held up for a prolonged period in the Duma; and strong political and military resistance to a START III seems guaranteed.

There is yet another menacing aspect of the danger posed to the world by the total stock of nuclear weapons. This is the fact that there are an estimated 5000 nuclear warheads on a status known as a 'hair-trigger alert' round the world. There are nuclear weapons states, notably the United States, which are ready to launch nuclear weapons within seconds as part of a 'launch on warning strategy'. In the event of an alert, it takes just three minutes to activate an Inter-Continental Ballistic Missile (ICBM) and virtually no time to send a Submarine-Launched Ballistic Missile (SLBM) on its way.[7]

START *Strategic Arms Reduction treaties*

In such a global environment, in a world still bristling with nuclear weapons, what is wrong with India (and Pakistan) going in for nuclear weapons? How would, say, an Indian stockpile of 24 to 36 nuclear warheads or even 150 warheads 10 to 15 years from now matter against many thousands of nuclear weapons worldwide?[8]

In order to answer this question seriously, we must first look at what nuclear weapons are, their character, and the imagination-defying dangers of annihilation they represent. At one level, this seems obvious enough. Yet the fact that nuclear weapons have been around for well over half a century, the sophisms of deterrence theory, and false claims made to the effect that nuclear weapons are political weapons meant not for use but for self-defence and national empowerment serve to inure public opinion to the real implications of producing, stockpiling, inducting, and deploying nuclear weapons, including several thousands on 'hair-trigger alert' status. Secondly, in order to answer the question, we must examine in some detail independent India's nuclear policy as it has evolved over five decades in response to perceived internal priorities and needs, to developing indigenous capabilities, and to changing international dynamics and contexts. If the policy is understood superficially or tendentiously interpreted (in the manner of some of the strategic affairs analysis, or rather apologia, that has fed into the BJP's chauvinist propaganda campaign on Pokhran-II and nuclear weaponization), a totally wrong conclusion, or wrong answer to a reasonable question, could follow.

WHAT IS A NUCLEAR BOMB?

The basic physical process that underlies the production of energy in nuclear reactors (research or power reactors) as well as nuclear weapons is the same, namely the fission of atomic nuclei. The basic difference between nuclear energy production and the nuclear bomb is that in the former, the process is strictly controlled, while in the latter it is allowed to proceed in an uncontrolled fashion. A useful analogy is provided by the production of energy from the combustion of petroleum products. Petrol, to take an example, is burned in a controlled way in an automobile engine to produce energy that propels the vehicle, but petrol in a container explodes when lit by a match.

Fundamental to both applications is the fact that atomic nuclei of elements of high atomic weight like uranium or plutonium undergo fission when struck by neutrons. When fission takes place, the nucleus splits into two nuclei (between which most of the neutrons and protons of the original nucleus are distributed) and one or more free neutrons. The difference in mass, which is really quite small, between the original nucleus and the end-products is manifested as the energy that is released. The energy released can be calculated using Einstein's celebrated formula $E=mc^2$, where E is the energy released, m is the difference in mass, and c is the velocity of light. Since the last quantity is an enormous number, the energy release from even the small mass difference per fission that takes place generates a relatively large amount of energy. The neutrons that are produced by fission can be made to strike other nuclei and the process is thus continued, creating what is referred to as a chain reaction. For the chain reaction to be sustained over a period of time, a minimum amount of fissile material, known as the critical mass, needs to be made available.

The difference between the bomb and the reactor lies in the difference in the growth rate in time of the net number of neutrons that are produced. In the case of the bomb, the 'over-critical' case, the number of neutrons available to induce further fission is required to grow rapidly, in fact exponentially. The energy release from the rapidly growing number of nuclei that fission is what constitutes the explosion of the atomic bomb. The situation is, in fact, quite the opposite in the case of the nuclear reactor. The number of neutrons available for further fission must *not* grow in time (except, obviously, when the reactor begins operation), but in fact must be produced at a constant rate (the 'critical' case). This is ensured by introducing other non-fissile material, referred to as a 'moderator', which is capable of absorbing neutrons. It would be very bad news if a reactor suddenly started to produce a growing number of neutrons. A good part of the essential safety aspect of nuclear reactor design consists in ensuring that this does not happen. The third situation, the 'sub-critical' case, is when the number of neutrons inducing further fission dies out over time. This is a situation that is of some importance in the testing of nuclear weapons.

The engineering requirements that are part of nuclear weapons construction are thus completely different from those associated with nuclear reactors. It follows that the data and information from nuclear weapons tests are useful only for nuclear weapons construction and not for any developmental work, in the common meaning of the term.

Another related question is whether the development of nuclear energy capabilities assists nuclear weapons development. The answer is a qualified 'yes'. The most important reason is that the knowledge of how to build nuclear reactors, whether for producing power or otherwise, provides access to the means of producing fissile material, particularly plutonium. But the presence of a nuclear power programme in a particular country does not automatically imply a covert nuclear weapons programme. It requires an independent commitment to develop such a technological capability.

Thermonuclear weapons or 'hydrogen bombs' use a completely different physical process for their functioning. As distinct from fission weapons, the explosive release of energy in this case is associated with the fusion of hydrogen nuclei to form nuclei of the inert gas helium. There is more than one reaction by which this fusion can be achieved. In the typical process used in modern thermonuclear weapons, a nucleus of the hydrogen isotope deuterium (containing one proton and one neutron) is made to fuse with the nucleus of another hydrogen isotope, tritium (which has one proton and two neutrons), to give a nucleus of helium (with two protons and two neutrons) and one free neutron. Excess energy is released because the mass of the helium nucleus plus the mass of the released neutron is less than the sum of the masses of the deuterium and tritium nucleus. It requires enormous temperature and pressure to force the deuterium and tritium nuclei sufficiently close together so that fusion takes place. This is typically achieved by using a fission explosion to create the required temperature and pressure conditions. Such fusion processes occur even in nature and are the primary source of the energy emitted by stars like the sun.

WEAPONS OF GENOCIDE

> If only, if *only,* nuclear war was just another kind of war. If only it was about the usual things – nations and territories, gods and histories. . . . If only nuclear war was the kind of war in which countries battle countries and men battle men. But it isn't. . . . Our foe will be the earth herself. The very elements – the sky, the air, the land, the wind and water – will all turn against us. Their wrath will be terrible. . . .

> What shall we do then, those of us who are still alive? Burned and blind and bald and ill, carrying the cancerous carcasses of our children in our arms, where shall we go? What shall we eat? What shall we drink? What shall we breathe?
>
> Arundhati Roy, 'The End of Imagination', a *Frontline* publication

In India, democratic and secular public opinion has always regarded nuclear weapons with horror, as weapons of mass destruction of a genocidal character. However, subsequent to the Pokhran and Chagai explosions, there has been a concerted effort by those in favour of nuclear weaponization to legitimize, even glorify, nuclear weapons as being acceptable means of achieving regional and global power. In the language currently in fashion among India's pro-bomb political figures, leading atomic energy and defence scientists, and instant experts of an assorted variety, bombs are 'devices' and nuclear weapons are 'weapons of deterrence'.

It is worthwhile therefore to recall the horrifying experiences of Hiroshima and Nagasaki. Over the past half century, knowledge of those acts of genocide by the United States has impelled millions of people in various parts of the world to protest against nuclear weapons. It has also made several thousands dedicate themselves to the task of nuclear disarmament.

Weapons of mass destruction are generally those that, when used, kill or otherwise devastate soldiers and civilians alike. As weapons of terror, they are often targetted primarily against civilians. Such weapons can be nuclear, chemical, or biological. Chemical weapons have been used in the past, although generally as extensions or modifications of conventional weapons; the worst are yet to be seen in action. Only nuclear weapons have been used in a way that is not substantially different in their effects from modern variants, aside from questions of scale. Despite protests of some of the scientists who worked on the development of nuclear weapons, the U.S. government decided to use the first bombs on the Japanese cities of Hiroshima and Nagasaki towards the end of the Second World War.

HIROSHIMA AND NAGASAKI

Hiroshima was bombed on August 6 and Nagasaki on August 9, 1945.[9] The bomb dropped on Hiroshima, which was of untested design and used approximately 64 kg of enriched uranium as fissile material, caused the death of over 200,000 people (as of October 1950). This was from an estimated 350,000 people present in the city on August 6. The bomb dropped on Nagasaki used 6.2 kg of plutonium and eventually killed 140,000 out of an estimated 270,000 people present in the city on August 9.

'Little Boy', as the Hiroshima bomb was endearingly code-named, had a yield of 15 kilotons equivalent of TNT. 'Fat Man', dropped on Nagasaki, had a yield of 21 kilotons. The result was devastation and death on a scale unknown before to humankind.

These bombs generated first an enormous fireball. The fireball radiates both heat and light. Surprisingly, the light did not cause too much damage, most of it being temporary, lasting from a few hours to a few days. Not many were looking directly at the sky in the direction of the explosion, the major cause of injury to the eye.

A nuclear weapon explosion also generates intense currents and electromagnetic fields, known as electromagnetic pulse or EMP, that does not damage living organisms but causes severe damage to electronic and electrical equipment over a wide area. In the case of a modern city, this would lead to immediate and total collapse of modern communications systems.

In an atmospheric nuclear weapon explosion, what causes the maximum damage is thermal radiation together with the shock wave that follows. At Hiroshima, people unshielded from thermal radiation suffered intense burns in a zone up to 1.5 km from ground zero. The thermal flash can cause spontaneous combustion of flammable objects and burn or char structures of wood, trees and so on. However, it does not lead to much self-sustained combustion except in some cases. What really helped set off the fires at Hiroshima and Nagasaki was the blast effect of the shock wave.

The shock wave begins near ground zero with speeds close to a hundred times the speed of sound. In the case of Nagasaki, the shock wave generated winds of over 1500 km per hour close to ground zero, while 3 km away it was still over 100 km per hour. Human beings are killed by objects hurtling around or from impact on hitting walls and other obstacles. Most buildings collapse in an extended zone around ground zero rendering them vulnerable to damage by fire. The fire is begun usually by heating appliances, kitchen fires and the like, and is aided considerably by the thermal wave that has just passed. Material scattered by the blast aid the rapid spread of the fire. The fire itself can develop in various ways. In Hiroshima, the fires began 20 minutes after the explosion. They built up into an intense fire with strong winds blowing into the fire area, known technically as a 'firestorm', with temperatures of up to several hundred degrees. At Nagasaki, it was a slow-starting, less intense fire, known as a 'conflagration', which lasted five hours.

Hiroshima and Nagasaki met this kind of devastation without warning. The civil defence system was immediately destroyed and survivors with serious injuries soon died. Fire-fighting was rendered impossible.

Radiation is, to a large extent, not a separate danger immediately after the blast. The range where radiation effects are lethal is equally dangerous for thermal and blast effects. Radioactive contamination is the chief cause of delayed deaths. The maximum danger comes from radioactive material of a wide variety that settles on the ground. This is called the 'fall-out'.

Radioactivity causes two types of effects. There are *acute* effects coming, typically, from rapid exposure; these effects show up in the short term (a few weeks). Then there are *latent* effects from prolonged exposure to relatively lower levels; these effects are manifested in the long term. At Hiroshima and Nagasaki deaths due to acute radiation sickness from severe exposure occurred within two weeks. Deaths in the cases of lesser exposure occurred six to eight weeks later. As for latent effects, cancer incidence increased, particularly the incidence of leukemia in the period between 1950 and 1953, and of other cancers later. Deaths due to radiation occurred even among those who entered the two cities much later, even 100 hours after the blast.

Radiation most affects those cells in the human body that replicate rapidly. Children and infants are thus more sensitive to radiation injury than adults, while fetuses are the most sensitive of all. Radiation can also have long-term genetic effects, damaging the gene pool of entire population groups. In the words of the eminent agricultural scientist and geneticist, M.S. Swaminathan, nuclear weapons also do damage to 'inter-generational equity'.[10]

There is now an enormous literature on the short-term and long-term effects of radioactive contamination, based not only on Hiroshima and Nagasaki data but also on the unwitting exposure of several individuals, groups and communities to the fall-out from nuclear testing particularly in the various islands in the Pacific used as testing grounds first by the United States and later by France.

Nuclear weapons also cause long-term damage to the environment. Full-scale global nuclear war can lead to long-term climatic change owing to the soot thrown up by burning cities, a phenomenon referred to as 'nuclear winter'. There are also effects on the soil and the ecosystem. Today, after a single explosion, there is no residual radioactivity at Hiroshima or Nagasaki. But the results may be different with explosions that are much closer to the ground, or with multiple explosions, both of which can lead to enhanced fall-out.

What are the lessons that Hiroshima and Nagasaki provide for the subcontinent? The combination of thermal and blast effects will be lethal in the Indian and Pakistani cities of today. Slums and areas of poor quality housing, with flimsy structures built out of easily combustible material, will be particularly vulnerable and buildings will be razed over a relatively large region. The blast effects will, in all probability, be seen farther out, with little to impede the shock wave.

An important study by scientist Rashid Naim has identified five major factors peculiar to South Asian countries that are relevant to this discussion.[11] The first factor is the higher population density in urban areas of South Asia. This will guarantee a higher number of casualties in the event of a nuclear explosion. Secondly, the limited fire-fighting capabilities in developing countries will greatly enhance the damage from thermal effects and fire. Thirdly, burn injuries that require immediate and sophisticated medical care will lead to much higher casualties on account of the low availability of such care in the region. Fourthly, economic resources in general and medical facilities in particular tend to be far more concentrated in urban areas in South Asia than in developed countries. With such facilities being incapacitated in a nuclear attack, there is little prospect of depending on the medical, shelter and economic facilities of peripheral areas and medium- and small-sized population centres to limit post-attack casualties. Fifthly, a large part of administrative, technical and industrial infrastructure is concentrated in a few areas in developing countries. This means that enormous damage can be done by very few warheads.

Another interesting study by an Indian physicist, M.V. Ramana, studies in detail the effects of nuclear weapons on the city of Mumbai.[12] Ramana's conclusions are chilling. The number of casualties estimated from mathematical models that extrapolate from the experience of Hiroshima and Nagasaki provide baseline data; in addition, particular local factors can exacerbate the damage. Modern cities contain far more explosive substances in daily use (such as gas cylinders in homes and the fuel of a large number of vehicles) than cities at the time of the Second World War. Mumbai is home to a large number of chemical factories; in the event of damage, they will additionally disperse toxic substances over a large region. As in some other parts of India, for example Chennai, there are nuclear installations close to the city. The catastrophe of a nuclear attack can be compounded many-fold if nuclear installations suffer damage.

Naim's study points out that in the event of nuclear weapons being used in the subcontinent, neither Pakistan or India will be spared the effects of the fall-out of radioactive material. The prevalent wind patterns over the subcontinent will ensure that the fall-out contaminates the soil and waters of both countries. Damage will be substantial in the border regions, particularly in the two Punjabs, regions that are of substantial economic and political significance for both countries.

Half a century after Hiroshima and Nagasaki, there exists no credible scheme of civil defence that can cope with a nuclear confrontation. Despite wild claims from some quarters in the Department of Atomic Energy, there is no way that India or Pakistan can even build shelters for their populations.[13] It is significant that even countries like the United States have given up on the idea.

In sum, it is extremely improbable that India and Pakistan will emerge from any kind of nuclear exchange as the nation states and civilizations they used to be.

With this, and much more readily available knowledge, the celebration of the nuclear bomb tests and the pride in nuclear weapons status witnessed in India and Pakistan, especially in the media and among the educated public, in the initial period following the Pokhran and Chagai explosions seem grotesque. The claim made by Prime Minister Vajpayee, speaking to a cheering crowd of BJP activists in front of his residence after Pokhran-II, that India would not hesitate 'to use these capabilities for self-defence', makes no scientific sense.[14]

Where exactly is an Indian government going to explode them in self-defence? Will it be in the Punjab? Or in Kashmir? If it is to be on foreign soil, will India remain uncontaminated by the fall-out?

Small wonder then that the survivors of Hiroshima and Nagasaki reacted with concern, alarm and outrage to news of the Indian and Pakistani nuclear tests and the chauvinistic celebrations that followed. Mariko Kitano, Islamic scholar from Osaka University and granddaughter of a Nagasaki survivor, was disgusted by the celebration she saw in Islamabad when the Pakistani tests were conducted. In an angry letter to a Pakistani newspaper, she described the scars she bears 'of that living hell' in her 'deformed feet, one eye that cannot see and a left hand that only lies motionless at my side'.[15] 'I am sickened to my stomach', she wrote, 'at the sight of these jubilant faces celebrating Pakistan's nuclear test. These are faces of unashamed ignorance. These are faces that have never even given a thought, let alone seen, the evil that is manifested in nuclear arms.'

IT COSTS A BOMB!

> . . . the recent nuclear events have added vastly to subcontinental tensions . . . it was . . . a great mistake . . . to undertake the nuclear tests. First of all, I think it was a big moral mistake. . . . But even at a more pragmatic, realpolitik level, there is no question that India has lost a lot from it . . . we don't know how much expenditure is incurred in nuclear war. But . . . the primary argument against the nuclear programme is not the economic cost.
>
> Amartya Sen, interview to Parvathi Menon in *Frontline*, January 15, 1999

How much did the United States spend on its nuclear weapons and weapons-related programme? A 'conservative' estimate is that between 1940 and 1996 the U.S. spent over $5.8 trillion (approx. Rs 249 lakh crores in end-March 1999 exchange rates), including the costs of storing and disposing of accumulating toxic and radioactive wastes, dismantling nuclear weapon systems, and disposing of surplus nuclear materials. This amounted to nearly 11 per cent of all government expenditures for the period, and exceeded all other categories of government spending except non-nuclear national defence and social security.[16]

What makes the nuclear weapons programme so expensive? There is far more to a nuclear weapons programme than merely successfully conducting tests or even producing nuclear bombs. Reddy lists the main elements of a weaponization programme:

assembling or producing nuclear warheads or bombs;

building or acquiring delivery systems; developing a command, control com-

INVESTMENT COST OF NUCLEAR WEAPONIZATION (*in Rs crore*)

One reactor to produce plutonium	700
One missile production facility	500
A 150-bomb arsenal	600
Missiles	
55 Prithvis	*385*
30 Agnis	*1,500*
25 Agni-IIs	*1,500*
16 Sagarikas	*640*
	4,025
Fitting one IAF squadron	60
Three n-submarines	12,000
Two satellites	2,000
C^3I	3,525+
Radar, missiles, etc., to protect airbases/launch sites	5,000
TOTAL	**28,000+**

Source C. Rammanohar Reddy, 'The wages of Armageddon-III', The Hindu, September 2, 1998.

munications and intelligence (C^3I) system, which will comprise a chain of command from the Prime Minister downwards;

fortified command and communications posts able to function under conditions of a nuclear attack;

satellite-based communications systems, and intelligence systems of various kinds;

establishing defence systems that will guard the nuclear delivery systems (in effect, air bases, missile launch sites, and submarines) from a conventional or nuclear attack.[17]

How much will the Indian weaponization programme cost? The Defence Ministry says Rs 2000 crores; MIND calculates the cost at Rs 40,000. General K. Sundarji, former Army Chief and a strong advocate of nuclear weaponization, gives a very 'affordable' figure of Rs 2760 crores (at 1996 prices), while Brigadier Vijai K. Nair estimates it to be Rs 6835 crores (projected in 1992 for a ten-year period). Both these latter estimates, as Reddy points out, have left out many components of actual nuclear weaponization and are gross underestimates. Sundarji, for example, left out C^3I in his 'broad brush calculation', explaining dismissively that 'such costs are common to conventional force requirements and are not to be taken as incremental costs'.

Reddy's own broad estimate of the investment costs of nuclear weaponization, defined as 'acquiring a second-strike capability comprising a triad delivery of 150 bombs', suggests something of the order of Rs 28,000 crores at current prices over a ten-year period for a triad delivery of 150 nuclear bombs. He notes that since this figure does not include all C^3I capital costs and for a number of other reasons, 'this is a large underestimate of the full burden of weaponization'. Once these costs are added on, 'the total financial demands of nuclear weaponization will be closer to a minimum of Rs 40,000 crores to Rs 50,000 crores over a 10 year period', that is Rs 4000 crores to Rs 5000 crores a year. This will consume 5 per cent of the Central Government's tax revenue every year, increase the total annual defence expenditure by about 10 per cent, and increase the annual defence capital outlay by about 30 per cent.

No matter how you calculate the cost, however, nuclear weaponization inevitably means diverting financial resources away from the basic needs of the Indian people. Money spent on

one nuclear bomb (Rs 4 crores) can finance the construction of 3200 houses for the rural poor under the Indira Awas Yojana;

each Agni missile (Rs 60 crores) can finance the annual operation of 15,000 grassroot rural primary health care centres;

setting up a missile production facility (Rs 500 crores) is twice what the Central Government will fund in 1998–99 for treating 750,000 hectares of rainfed area under the watershed development programme;

producing an arsenal of 150 bombs (Rs 600 crores) can provide drinking water to 37,000 villages under the accelerated rural water supply scheme;

150 bombs is the same as the total Central Government Budget outlay on public health in 1998–99, i.e. the expenditure on control of leprosy, malaria, tuberculosis and AIDS;

one nuclear dyad strike force (Rs 4000 crores) is more than the Central Government Budget outlay on elementary and secondary education in 1998–99;

one nuclear-powered submarine (Rs 4000 crores) is the same as the cost of setting up a 1000 Mw power plant;

one triad strike force (Rs 2500 crores plus) is approximately the same as what the Central Government spends on elementary education every year;

the full nuclear weaponization programme – Rs 40,000 crores to Rs 50,000 crores – can be used to remove the entire rural housing shortage estimated at 15 million units in 1991; or it can be used to set in place an educational system that provides primary education for all Indian children of school-going age.

Then there are other invisible costs. The economist Jayati Ghosh raises pertinent issues relating to the different costs of nuclear weaponization, including the-hard-to-estimate indirect costs flowing from the erosion of economic sovereignty and independence, and the problem of anti-democratic 'opacity' of government expenditure on nuclear weaponization.[18]

This is the true burden of a nuclear weapons programme on the people of India.

3

DETTERENCE THEORY AND NUCLEAR THEOLOGY

We are told that nuclear weapons are necessary as a deterrent against war and that it is only the assurance of their use that constitutes the core of deterrence. We do not accept that thesis. We believe that nuclear weapons are dangerous whether they are in the possession of one country, some countries or many countries. We are not only against the proliferation of nuclear weapons, we are against nuclear weapons themselves.

Speech of External Affairs Minister A.B. Vajpayee on October 4, 1977 at the 32nd Session, 18th Plenary Meeting of the United Nations General Assembly, New York

The concept of a security system of which nuclear weapons represent the most dangerous and totally unacceptable component must be abandoned.

Speech of External Affairs Minister A.B. Vajpayee on October 10, 1978 at the 33rd Session, 29th Plenary Meeting of the United Nations General Assembly, New York

The nuclear weapon is not an offensive weapon. It is a weapon of self-defence. It is the kind of weapon that helps in preserving the peace. If in the days of the Cold War there was no use of force, it was because of the balance of terror.

Reply by Prime Minister A.B. Vajpayee on March 15, 1999 in the Lok Sabha to the debate on the motion of thanks to the President[1]

In any civilized world view, weapons of mass destruction are indefensible as instruments of state policy. This applies above all to nuclear weapons, the ultimate means of mass annihilation. After all, humanity had a practical demonstration on August 6 and 9, 1945 of what atom bombs can do to people and to civilization. How then to justify the unjustifiable? It was to perform this task that the doctrine of deterrence made its appearance as the mainstay of arguments in favour of nuclear weapons. Often camouflaged by the trappings of science, the theory of nuclear deterrence rests on a number of assumptions that are either questionable or demonstrably false, so much so that some critics give it the appellation, 'nuclear theology'.

Before we explore the specifics of deterrence, we shall trace the path by which the doctrine has come to play the role it does in strategic affairs and international politics. The manner in which this happened is elegantly described in two books, *The Abolition* by Jonathan Schell, and *Weapons of Hope* by the physicist Freeman Dyson.[2] At the end of the Second World War, when the world had only one nuclear weapons state – the United States – the question of deterrence did not arise. But the 'danger' arising from the acquisition of the bomb by several countries, notably the socialist Soviet Union, was quickly realized by scientists, political leaders and other thinkers. It was imperative, the physicist Niels Bohr said, to put in place some international mechanism by which these weapons could be controlled. A series of moves initiated by Bohr and Robert Oppenheimer culminated in the Acheson–Lilenthal report on the international control of nuclear energy. The report was prepared by a committee at the instance of the then U.S. Secretary of State, James Byrnes. The final form of these disarmament proposals, often referred to as the Baruch Plan, presented to the United Nations in July 1946 sought patently to preserve the technological lead of the United States rather than pursue genuine disarmament.[3] The plan, which ignored national sovereignty in a manner that was to become characteristic of the U.S. non-proliferation agenda in subsequent years, proposed international ownership under the United Nations of all dangerous aspects of nuclear energy-related activities, from the mining of uranium onwards. In a parallel move, the plan proposed the suspension of the veto in the Security Council on the nuclear issue. Given a UN dominated by the United States, this would have come close to total control over nuclear weapons for the indefinite future.

The Soviet Union rejected the Baruch Plan and responded with a radical set of relatively simple proposals. It called for, first, banning the production of nuclear weapons. This was to be followed by discussions to reach agreement on safeguards for the abolition agreement and on peaceful scientific co-operation. The correctness of this approach is evident today, considering that the Chemical Weapons Convention (CWC), a complex treaty that was opened for signature in early 1993 and entered into force on April 29, 1997, is based on a similar approach.

The United States rejected these proposals out of hand. It chose instead to try and overwhelm the Soviet Union through technological superiority. The first socialist state responded by racing to catch up in an era when the United States and its allies were attempting to contain it by all means. Dyson notes objectively: 'Today with hindsight, we may equally lament the great opportunity that was missed when the United States rejected the Soviet prohibition treaty.'[4]

The nuclear arms race and spiral that resulted, and their staggering economic costs, are well-known.[5] It is the ideological attempt in western countries to rationalize and justify the induction, stockpiling and deployment of nuclear weapons that has given the doctrine of deterrence the elevated status it has had during the past half century.

The original idea behind the doctrine of deterrence is found in two chapters of a 1946 book, *The Absolute Weapon*, written by the political scientist Bernard Brodie. In a key passage, Brodie asserted: 'Multilateral possession of the bomb, therefore, will discourage, not encourage, aggression, provided that it is as nearly certain as possible that the aggressor who uses the bomb will have it used against him.' From this core idea, as Schell points out, follows the rest of the theory of deterrence:

While nuclear weapons offer nations unlimited force, nuclear war itself is unwinnable.

The main aim of strategy is to stop such a war from ever beginning.

It is the possession of nuclear weapons that will help ensure that nuclear war does not take place.

It is particularly important to possess a retaliatory nuclear strike capability that is invulnerable.

There is special danger if either side possesses the capability to destroy the nuclear forces of the other side in a first-strike.

'Perceptions' and 'psychology' play an essential role in convincing the adversary that any aggression by him will lead only to his annihilation. This draws the adversary into maintaining the stability of the whole arrangement.

The threat of nuclear annihilation was not a particular concern for deterrence theory. What was essential was that both sides build up such a capability that the other would be deterred. Once a sufficient level of nuclear arms was reached by either side and strategic parity attained, the situation would become 'stable'. The fact that the world would teeter on the brink of an abyss in such a situation was taken for granted. Peace and stability would be guaranteed precisely because it was in neither side's interest to see this precarious balance disturbed. In the view of the original proponents of this doctrine, this was to be a temporary solution while the deeper problem of abolishing nuclear weapons could be dealt with suitably.

In practice, of course, such hopes were quickly laid to rest. Subsequently, the doctrine of deterrence has acquired many trappings and has been extended in several different ways, spawning an enormous literature. Deterrence first threw out of sync the U.S. strategic doctrine known as 'massive retaliation', that is, a large-scale nuclear attack on the Soviet Union as a response to non-nuclear 'Communist aggression' against the U.S. or its allies.[6] A cerebral future U.S. Secretary of State, Henry Kissinger, was to make his name in Cold War political circles with an influential and stylishly written book on the role of nuclear weapons in foreign policy.[7] Here he questioned what passed for strategic doctrine in the 1950s, but not the theology of deterrence. This neo-conservative treatise bolstered the view among Cold Warriors that it was not 'the type of explosive or the explosive power' (to quote from Gordon Dean's foreword to the book) that was immoral or unacceptable; it was 'the use' to which nuclear weapons were put that made the action moral or immoral, acceptable or unacceptable.

Soon after Kissinger's book came out, it became clear that 'massive retaliation' was not a viable doctrine. Growing Soviet capability to retaliate against U.S. territory seemed to guarantee a general nuclear war, or 'World War III', in the event of any U.S. nuclear attack on its chief adversary.

Deterrence theory also yielded peculiar conclusions when the reasoning behind it was carried through. For instance, the building of a large civil defence infrastructure was, in principle, not acceptable.[8] Building an infrastructure in one country might enable it to gain a greater degree of invulnerability, thus 'destabilizing' deterrence. Allowing one's own population to be hostage to the nuclear weapons of the other side was an essential aspect of the theology of deterrence. It was, of course, impossible in practice to completely ignore the question of civil defence. But what is indisputable is that barring possibly China (with its extensive underground nuclear shelters belonging to a bygone era and now converted to other uses), the nuclear weapons states have not done what they could have done to 'protect' more than a fraction of their population in the event of a nuclear confrontation.

How is one to know that deterrence works? The classic answer has been to point to the fact that during the Cold War the United States and the Soviet Union never directly fought a war, much less a war with nuclear weapons. This is supposed to be the basic proof that deterrence has worked.

The problems with this flawed, contradictory, and abhorrent theory were more than moral, as was realized from the very beginning. As Schell points out, the first to realize this were the western strategists of nuclear war.[9] It was all very well to commend the stability conferred by 'strategic parity' when the United States was ahead. But once the Soviet Union caught up with the U.S. in technological terms and even threatened to get ahead (when its space programme took off in the second half of the 1950s, scoring some stunning firsts), no Cold War strategist was willing to put his money on such 'stability'. Once the 'assured destruction' of the Soviet Union turned into a scenario of mutual assured destruction (MAD), the first concern for imperialist strategists was the 'defence' of Europe.[10] Deterrence, they feared in an argument typical of the paranoid, hyper-rational world of deterrence theory, would embolden the Soviets to attack Europe without fear of retaliation.

The result was the development of the ideas of 'limited nuclear war' and 'flexible response', which, it was suggested, would allow the United States and its allies to retaliate against the threat of Soviet 'aggression' with short-range nuclear missiles without putting into play the full force of western nuclear arsenals. But it soon became obvious that there was no scenario in which a 'limited' nuclear exchange would not lead to total nuclear war. Nor were the people of Europe enthused by the idea of the United States using their soil as the ground for a nuclear confrontation.

As Schell points out, the chief concern eventually became not making deterrence work, but what to do in the event that 'deterrence failed' or in the event of the 'breakdown of deterrence'.[11] Or as Kissinger put it: 'Perhaps the basic problem of strategy in the nuclear age is how to establish a relationship between a policy of deterrence and a strategy for fighting a war in case deterrence fails'.[12] In the heyday of Reaganism and the 'Star Wars' programme, when there were several indications that the economic and political system of the Soviet Union was getting into trouble, the emphasis shifted transiently to 'winning', or 'prevailing in', a nuclear war. Among other things, the delusions associated with 'Star Wars' showed that those who were in charge of nuclear weapons in the western world had virtually given up on deterrence.

A fundamental flaw of deterrence theory is the assumption that once both sides build up their nuclear arsenals to a threshold level, matters will stabilize. Continued acquisition of new technological capabilities put paid to that idea. As newer technologies emerged, fresh possibilities opened up, driven often by the weapons establishments simply seeking to try out their newest ideas and finding means to do so. New technology fuelled the arms race, leading to the monstrous overkill capacity of increasingly sophisticated nuclear arsenals.

There is a fundamental contradiction at the core of deterrence theory. Possessing nuclear weapons commits a state that has them to perform, in certain circumstances, insane actions that must never be done under any circumstances – because they will plunge the world into a nuclear holocaust. The benefit that is to be gained, according to the argument of deterrence, is that by threatening to perform an insane action, one will never have to perform it. This absurdity will seem to work until an actual crisis point is reached. But it cannot be admitted in advance that at the moment of crisis sanity will prevail and the weapons will not be used – because that is to lose the benefits enjoyed prior to the breakdown of deterrence. In the end, the bottom line is not that peace will prevail and that war will be set aside by the possession of nuclear weapons. The stark truth is that the possessor stands committed to threatening to use, and actually using, nuclear weapons.

But even more than these theoretical arguments, it is the truth about the world as it really was during the Cold War era that debunks the theory of deterrence. One of the gravest dangers of nuclear war developed out of the confrontation triggered by U.S. imperialism that is known as the 'Cuban missile crisis'. The crisis was resolved because both the Soviet Union and the United States gave up substantial ground. A remarkable admission of the hollowness of deterrence theory comes from Robert McNamara, Defence Secretary under the Kennedy and Johnson administrations, in an interview to Schell:

> Even a low possibility of catastrophe is a high risk, and I don't think we should continue to accept it. If you don't believe it's a risk, then read the reports of the Cuban Missile Crisis Retrospective Meetings and the recently published Kennedy tapes. I believe that was the best-managed Cold War crisis of any, but we came within a hairbreadth of nuclear war without realizing it. There were mistakes made by Khruschev and his associates, and by Kennedy and his associates, including me. We made miscalculations, misjudgments, in what I call the best-managed crisis. It's no credit to us that we missed nuclear war – at least, we had to be lucky as well as wise. So I want to say that's a risk I don't believe the human race should accept.[13]

The most important testimony to the fact that 'peace' in the Cold War period had nothing to do with deterrence comes from General Lee Butler, former Commander of the U.S. Strategic Forces, that is, the man who for several years commanded the nuclear arsenal of the United States. 'Deterrence never really worked', is the central message of General Butler's interview to Schell.[14]

First of all, deterrence never led to stability. Being invulnerable to a first-strike was an essential requirement of deterrence. Even one nuclear weapon could not be allowed to get through a country's defences, because the consequences would be catastrophic. 'But your perfect invulnerability would spell perfect vulnerability for your opponent, which of course he cannot accept. Consequently, any balance struck is extremely unstable, and each side is led to build larger and larger arsenals, to discover more and more elegant technologies.'

Secondly, 'deterrence fails at the psychological level'. The so-called psychological dimension of deterrence never worked in practice in the Cold War relationship between the United States and the Soviet Union. Why? According to General Butler, the explanation lay in the 'lack of dialogue, a conviction that each harboured the most hostile possible motivations toward the other. And, consequently, a set of war plans that were premissed on worst-case assumptions and outcomes'. The tendency to 'demonize each other, to reduce to caricatures each other's motivations, intentions and beliefs' flew in the face of 'the detailed, sophisticated understanding that deterrence requires in order to operate, especially in a crisis'.

Thirdly, in General Butler's view, deterrence in practice was 'turned on its head'. Whatever one side did by way of developing and making evident the capability of a retaliatory threat looked to the other side, 'through the prism of your enemy's perspective', to be suspiciously like an increase in first-strike capability, and vice versa. Despite the theoretical claims, when deterrence was made real and operationalized in terms of actual weapons and delivery systems, it achieved exactly the opposite of what was claimed, stable security. 'Thus, your quest for security, by building a highly credible deterrent force, is *unhinged* by your opponent's need to respond in kind. In my view, that paradox is the fundamental problem at an operational level with deterrence'.

Deterrence was an ideological–political construct which arose at an early stage of the Cold War and served imperialism for many decades despite abundant theoretical and empirical evidence that it could not be relied upon. Deterrence theory depended crucially on its ability to predict the behaviour of the adversary. But as General Butler points out, the Soviet Union did not view its nuclear weapons in the way the theory predicts. For instance, it paid far greater attention than the United States to the protection of its command and control, and several key elements of infrastructure, against nuclear attack. The former commander of the U.S. Strategic Forces acknowledges that, in the background of the ideological and political confrontation the United States pursued with the Soviet state, U.S. nuclear weapons represented an aggressive threat to the Soviet Union until it attained strategic nuclear parity.

Asked by his interviewer to respond to the contention that the nuclear arsenals of the two global powers 'kept the peace' and 'prevented World War III' during the Cold War period, General Butler points out that in order to establish that that contention is true, one has to first establish that such a war was at all intended or likely to break out. There is no evidence, he concludes, that the Soviet Union actually ever intended to attack the United States or its allies in Europe. It was the experience of the Cuban missile crisis, during which rival negotiators were 'groping frantically in an intellectual fog, in the dark, to deal with a crisis that had spun out of control', that convinced both sides that caution was absolutely necessary if they were not to find themselves at annihilating war.

More is known today than ever before about the dangers represented by nuclear weapons, including the risks of their accidental or unauthorized use.[15] While deterrence theory proclaims the virtues of possessing and deploying, but not using, nuclear weapons, in practice the possibility of unauthorized and accidental use remains unacceptably high. This danger is compounded by the deployment of a large number of tactical nuclear weapons round the world. In a crisis, if communication with the main command and control centres is broken, there is a real possibility of launch on local authority. Such situations arose during the Cuban missile crisis. There have been several documented instances of accident situations that have brought nuclear weapons close to launch. The most recent close call came in 1995, when a stray weather rocket from Norway was for a while suspected by the Russian military to be a missile. The 'nuclear briefcase' that Russian Presidents carry to authorize the launch of nuclear weapons was readied for President Boris Yeltsin's use until it was determined that the alarm was false.[16]

Let us note, in conclusion, that the possession of nuclear weapons has proved to be of little avail in conventional conflicts. The nuclear arsenal of the United States was powerless to stop the liberation and unification of Vietnam and the liberation of Cambodia and Laos. The possession of nuclear weapons was of no use to the Soviet Union in its costly misadventure in Afghanistan. The menacing entry of a nuclear-armed U.S. naval task force led by the aircraft carrier *Enterprise* into the Bay of Bengal during the 1971 war of liberation of Bangladesh could not influence the course of events in any material way. This incident is frequently cited by pro-weaponization analysts in India to make the case for nuclear weaponization. However, it is clear that the correct and legitimate Indian stand on the Bangladesh liberation issue and the overwhelming support that it had from domestic and world public opinion proved more than a match for any implied nuclear threat.

INDIAN POLICY AND THE DETERRENT

Until the Pokhran-II misadventure, official Indian policy ranged itself firmly and eloquently against the doctrine of nuclear deterrence. This opposition goes back to the early days of the Indian nuclear programme and policy. More recently, an Indian memorial submitted to the International Court of Justice in 1995 on the question of the legality of nuclear weapons was a stinging indictment of the doctrine.[17] The memorial argued:

> The use of nuclear weapons in response to attack by a conventional weapon would patently violate the principle of proportionality, but also a nuclear response to a nuclear attack would violate the principle of discrimination, humanity, environmental security and probably the principle of neutrality as such an attack would not distinguish between combatants and non-combatants – causing civilian casualties, ravaging the natural environment and contaminating the territory of neighbouring and distant neutral countries. *Nuclear deterrence has been considered to be abhorrent to human sentiment* since it implies that a state if required to defend its own existence will act with pitiless disregard for the consequences to its own and its adversary's people. [Emphasis added]

The Indian memorial addressed the question of whether the doctrinc of deterrence was justified in the light of the argument that nuclear weapons would never actually be used. It argued that 'those who do not have such weapons would all the time be racing to build them and those who already have nuclear weapons to maintain the superiority necessary for deterrence and this would keep humanity in the perpetual fear of total destruction'.

This principled position has been completely overturned with Pokhran-II and Chagai. Predictably, a chorus of apologists in the strategic affairs community and in the media have intoned the virtues of deterrence, projecting wild scenarios that have no basis in reality even by the standards of deterrence theory.[18] Even the historical record needs to be altered, not so subtly, to suit the present. Two recent Indian strategic affairs articles included in *Nuclear India* and devoted to 'Five Decades of Nuclear Weapons' and India's 'long struggle for nuclear disarmament over the last 50 years' completely edit out of the record the pre-Pokhran-II official Indian opposition to deterrence theory.[19]

The new-found official fascination with the logic of deterrence marks a low point in the history of India's nuclear policy. It represents an abject acceptance of the cast-off intellectual rags of the U.S. nuclear weapons establishment at a time when the theory of deterrence has begun to be questioned even by those who once held leadership roles in its practice. Speaking in the Lok Sabha on March 15, 1999, Prime Minister Vajpayee broke into a paean of praise for deterrence in the context of nuclear weaponization in South Asia:

> Now both India and Pakistan are in possession of nuclear weapons. There is no alternative but to live in mutual harmony. The nuclear weapon is not an offensive weapon. It is a weapon of self-defence. *It is the kind of weapon that helps in preserving the peace.* If in the days of the Cold War there was no use of force, it was because of the balance of terror. One side could have given in and one side established dominance. But that never happened. [Emphasis added]

Nuclear weapons were now seen as a positive spur to the talking:

> We wish to discuss all issues with Pakistan and work out appropriate solutions. We have had three conflicts in fifty years. Now we have to devise ways of stopping wars for all time. There is no way to do this but the way of dialogue. Whatever the issue, we are prepared to talk it over.[20]

Vajpayee had evidently never read Bertrand Russell's classic *Common Sense and Nuclear Warfare*,[21] not to mention J.B. Priestley's stirring articles in the *New Statesman* in the 1950s, invoking the image of 'rabbits waiting for the massacre' and calling on the British people to 'defy this nuclear madness into which the spirit of Hitler seems to have passed, to poison the world'.[22] Nor did he seem familiar with the devastating refutation of deterrence theory by the great British historian A.J.P. Taylor.[23]

Applying his insight into the causes of world wars to the challenge posed by nuclear weapons, Taylor began by observing matter-of-factly: 'The prime cause of the [First World] War lay in the precautions that had been taken to ensure that there would be no war. The deterrent dominated strategical planning before 1914. The deterrent did not prevent war: it made war inevitable'. He then turned fiercely on the doctrine of the nuclear deterrent:

> I deplore the historians who, against all past experience, declare that this time the deterrent in the shape of nuclear weapons will preserve peace for ever. The deterrent starts off only as a threat, but the record shows that there comes a time when its reality has to be demonstrated – which can only be done by using it. So it was in August 1914 and so it will be again. So far we have done very well. We have lived under nuclear terror for forty years and are still here. The danger increases every day. Without the abolition of nuclear weapons the fate of mankind is certain . . . for ordinary people there still remain standards of right and wrong. One of these is that no country, no political system, is entitled to employ mass murder in order to maintain itself.

Counterpose to this historian's warning Vajpayee's end-of-the-twentieth century celebration of the bomb – 'It is the kind of weapon that helps in preserving the peace' – and you have yet another text-book case of *akratic* adherence to a chauvinistic ideology driving away common sense.

We shall specifically examine, in a later section, the South Asian avatar of deterrence – the 'minimum credible nuclear deterrent' – that is supposed to guarantee India's security and usher in a new era of peace and stability in the subcontinent.

4

SUBVERTING INDIA'S NUCLEAR POLICY

In a classic exercise in doublespeak, Prime Minister Vajpayee used an early magazine interview opportunity to try and appeal to two seemingly incompatible political constituencies on the nuclear issue.[1] On the one hand, he suggested to the Hindutva constituency that only the BJP, 'guided by long-term imperatives based on a sound appraisal of regional and global security realities' and with 'the supreme consideration of national interests' at heart, had had the guts to do what Prime Minister Indira Gandhi had once boldly attempted, only to be stopped in her tracks. On the other hand, he acknowledged, with an eye to a broader political constituency for Pokhran-II, that every government and every Prime Minister of independent India had kept 'India's nuclear option open' and supported 'India's indigenous research and development in the nuclear field'. What the BJP-led government was doing, according to Vajpayee, was to 'build the superstructure on that solid foundation'; he also said that 'my Government's policy is consistent with the nuclear disarmament policy that successive governments have followed'.

Were the May 1998 Pokhran explosions the culmination of a natural Indian nuclear policy evolution or progression? Or did they represent a departure from that policy?

There can be no question that India's nuclear policy was built on sound and progressive lines laid down in the late 1940s by Homi Bhabha, the distinguished physicist and founding chairman of the Atomic Energy Commission, and Prime Minister Jawaharlal Nehru. The relatively early development of a multi-faceted nuclear programme was part of the process of industrialization in India. It drew on an important human resource, an Indian community of pure physicists and mathematicians that emerged in the 1940s. The programme gained strength from a substantial institute of fundamental research, a nuclear energy statute, a nuclear science establishment with an imaginative leadership, and the growth of sophisticated scientific and technical expertise that gained from increasing interaction with international science and technology. Finally, the programme benefited from the availability of natural resources as well as a fairly sophisticated (but still problematical) industrial and technological base for the relevant development.[2] The need to get the balance right between the peaceful scientific uses of atomic energy and its military potential, and to create and empower through carefully crafted legislation an effective atomic energy establishment, figured in the Constituent Assembly debates of 1948, drawing strong support from virtually all parts of the political spectrum.[3]

The substance of the Indian policy that took shape early in the international history of nuclear energy development was to pursue a many-sided nuclear energy programme that would be committed to the peaceful, non-military uses of nuclear energy, but would retain its independence within the larger context of working politically towards the goal of universal nuclear disarmament. Historically, the motivations for the policy have been two-fold. First, there were the general attractions of a high yield field in which the investment, although demanding, could be managed incrementally, especially if the programme could count on significant foreign assistance and technical cooperation in its less developed phases. Secondly, there was the attraction of nuclear power as a viable and prestigious proposition in a country that had been chronically deficient in terms of the total energy requirement at all points in its independent career. Some time during the course of the 1960s, a third motivation surfaced in the course of the development of the research side of the programme. Marked by ambiguity and somewhat conflicting interpretations, this was codeworded India's 'nuclear option'. Its basic content was nuclear weapons capability, which the programme certainly attained by the early 1970s.

Thus the policy had two basic elements: (1) the pursuit of independence and the refusal to accept any external controls and restraints instituted in a discriminatory way; and (2) a voluntary commitment to the peaceful, non-military uses of nuclear energy and, therefore, conditional self-restraint in not exercising the sovereign option of making nuclear weapons and deploying them.[4] It could be described as a policy of 'walking on two legs'.

As the unequal and discriminatory global nuclear regime gradually took shape over the 1950s and 60s, India's policy was clearly one of opposition to it. But before India arrived at this stance, it undertook several political and diplomatic initiatives, notably in 1965, to check and halt the escalation of nuclear weapons (initiatives that the best-known among Indian strategic affairs analysts, K. Subrahmanyam, a longstanding advocate of nuclear weaponization, characterizes as demonstrating 'a certain amount of naivete.')[5]

The United States, having developed nuclear weapons and actually used them, had for some four years an absolute monopoly over nuclear weapons. But the situation changed profoundly when the Soviet Union (rejecting the self-serving U.S.-sponsored Baruch Plan) demonstrated itself to be a nuclear weapons state in 1949. The knowledge and technology of nuclear science proliferated rapidly. Soon, the United Kingdom (1952), France (1960), and socialist China (1964) became acknowledged nuclear weapons states.

As the arms race proceeded apace, the dream of nuclear disarmament receded and was increasingly seen as utopian. Preventing horizontal proliferation of nuclear weapons and also sensitive nuclear – 'threshold' – capabilities became the principal western objective. Beginning in the 1950s, a succession of discriminatory non-proliferation initiatives, revolving round the divine right of the United States and its chosen allies to use nuclear weapons for 'self-defence', failed to make much headway in the face of Soviet and subsequently Chinese opposition to their purpose and orientation.

Then, following the positive breakthrough represented by the 1963 partial test ban treaty, negotiations for a non-proliferation treaty took off. The Treaty on the Non-Proliferation of Nuclear Weapons, under serious negotiation from 1965, was concluded and opened up for signature in 1968, rushed through the United Nations General Assembly (UNGA), and brought into force in 1970.

Its essence was the permanent division of the world into five nuclear weapons states, the 'haves', and the rest, the 'have-nots'. By defining a nuclear weapons state as 'one which has manufactured and exploded a nuclear weapon or other explosive device prior to 1 January, 1967' and prohibiting any signatory other than the five members of the pre-NPT nuclear weapons club from possessing nuclear weapons or 'other nuclear explosive devices', the NPT vested the former with superior rights.

The independence of Indian nuclear policy came under test during the run-up to the NPT. India's dependence on concessional food imports and aid from the United States made its government extremely vulnerable to intense western political pressure. It also looked to the Soviet Union for concessional military supplies and aid. During the 'considerable debate' that took place on the NPT, while 'a large section of the political class, bureaucracy, media and academia were doubtful' about India's ability to withstand external pressure, the government of Prime Minister Indira Gandhi made the crucial decision to stay out of the NPT.[6]

Since 1970, this discriminatory regime has been extended every five years in NPT review conferences envisioned by Article VIII of the treaty. In May 1995, the New York Review and Extension Conference, convened under Article X(2), decided to extend the treaty indefinitely and without conditions – thus making the DGNB a permanent feature of international politics. With 185 countries, including the two late-comer nuclear weapons states, France and China, becoming parties to the NPT, only three 'threshold' states with significant nuclear weapons capabilities – India, Pakistan and Israel – remain outside.

While the discriminatory regime has been perpetuated, the vague promise contained in the non-binding statement of intent and objectives to 'achieve at the earliest possible date the cessation of the nuclear arms race and to undertake effective measures in the direction of nuclear disarmament,' has been given the go-by.

NPT *Nuclear Non-Proliferation Treaty* DGNB *Discriminatory Global Nuclear Bargain*

THE NUCLEAR OPTION AND THE 1974 PNE

Until May 1974, the Indian nuclear energy programme benefited from substantial international cooperation, the supply from abroad of nuclear reactors, components and special material, opportunities for scientific study, research and training abroad, and international scientific contacts. During this period, the United States, Canada, the Soviet Union and France made significant inputs into the development of the programme. To handle these relationships, nuclear policy worked out for its own guidance clear *rules for the game* that kept the independent element and the peaceful-developmental element in balance and thus stood the country in good stead. The key element in these rules, which bear the authoritative stamp of the founder of the nuclear programme, Homi Bhabha, is India's refusal to accept 'full-scope safeguards', that is, external controls and restrictions on all its nuclear installations and the whole gamut of its nuclear energy activities. India's opposition to 'full-scope safeguards' is tied to its opposition to the discriminatory NPT regime. So also the refusal to accept other 'NPT equivalents' like the U.S.-sponsored demand to declare South Asia a nuclear weapons-free zone. This opposition to the NPT regime was backed by a strong national political consensus, even if vacillations did surface occasionally, as during the Morarji Desai Prime Ministership of 1977–79.[7]

The antecedents of Pokhran-I of May 18, 1974 are complex and somewhat hazy. However, Bhabha's restlessness after China's explosion of a nuclear weapon in October 1964 is documented.[8] With Prime Minister Nehru dead, the mood at the top levels of the ruling party ran in favour of developing a nuclear weapons programme, although there was no clarity about the consequences and implications of such a step. Bhabha's response to a fluid situation was to call a press conference in London the same month.[9] After making some philosophical observations about the nature of nuclear deterrence and the acquisition of 'the capability and threat of retaliation' as 'the only defence' against a nuclear attack, he formulated for the first time in public India's nuclear option: 'We are still 18 months away from exploding either a bomb or a device for peaceful purposes, and we are doing nothing to reduce that period'. According to one insider's account, the founder-leader of India's atomic energy establishment was

PNE *peaceful nuclear explosion/experiment* **NPT** *Nuclear Non-Proliferation Treaty*

'immediately rebuked by V.K. Krishna Menon, who was a fervent anti-nuclear campaigner'.[10]

In the wake of the Chinese nuclear test, views were expressed within the Ministries of External Affairs and Defence, and also at senior levels of the Congress party, in favour of an Indian nuclear weapons programme. Prime Minister Lal Bahadur Shastri resisted the pressure, but made some modifications to nuclear policy, notably by sanctioning Bhabha's proposal to look into a 'Subterranean Nuclear Explosion Project'.[11] Less than two years after Bhabha's London press conference, land was acquired in Rajasthan by the Government of India to provide a new 'artillery test range' and this became the Pokhran nuclear test range.

With the 'Peaceful Nuclear Explosion' (PNE) experiment of May 1974, it became clear to the whole world that India was a nuclear weapons capable state. After some lag, it became clear that Pakistan was also a nuclear weapons capable state.

The question of what original event or process began this competitive quest for nuclear weapons capability in South Asia is disputable. There is a small corpus of journalistic and non-proliferation literature that suggests that following its debacle in the 1971 war over Bangladesh's liberation, the Pakistani government began a top priority secret programme to develop a nuclear weapons capability to match India's suspected capability.[12] However, there can be little doubt that the first Pokhran explosion had the effect of intensifying, in 1974–75, the Zulfikar Ali Bhutto regime's effort to develop a uranium enrichment centrifuge facility at Kahuta and acquire nuclear weapons capability. Islamabad was particularly annoyed that, as a direct consequence of the Indian PNE, western nuclear suppliers imposed an embargo on nuclear exports to Pakistan.

According to the leaders of the Indian nuclear energy programme, it has always had a content and depth that Pakistan's has lacked; and it has stayed consistently ahead. But when it came to nuclear weapons capability and the nuclear option, there was understood to be a rough equivalence. Some strategic affairs analysts spoke about the existence of a 'non-weaponized' deterrence (in some readings, even a 'recessed deterrence') in South Asia. But whatever it was, non-weaponization of the two nuclear options helped to hold the balance in favour of peace and stability. Conversely, the weaponization option was always understood by democratic, progressive and indeed any sober political thinking to be destabilizing and costly.

In the context of what happened to the policy in the hands of the government of the Hindu Right, conceptual clarity about what the nuclear option was, why it had to be retained and developed, what the conditions were under which it would not be exercised, and what its motivations and purposes were become vitally important. From a democratic and progressive standpoint, the pursuit of independence on the nuclear question needs to go hand in hand with non-hawkishness, self-restraint, and a genuine commitment to the global de-legitimization and elimination of nuclear weapons. This is the polar opposite of the Jaswant Singh–Arun Shourie line of favouring one set of rules while standing outside the crowded railway compartment and supporting when inside 'the rules that will keep you in and keep the others out'.

Since Independence, India has been calling for global nuclear disarmament and Indian diplomacy has launched or pursued many worthwhile initiatives towards this end. Over the years, although the country faced many pressures intended to make it fall in line with the Discriminatory Global Nuclear Bargain, it did manage to resist them and to refuse to capitulate to the bargain while retaining its original commitment to disarmament. The retention of the nuclear option must be seen in this context.

In the post-1974 period, India's posture and actions on the nuclear option were characterized by a mixture of conditional self-restraint and resistance towards the arm-twisting 'non-proliferation' efforts spearheaded by the United States. Despite the obstructions, pressures and vacillations, national policy succeeded in preserving its commitment to the peaceful, non-military uses of nuclear energy while refusing to sign away the sovereignty of national decision-making on the issue.

Until the BJP-led government came along, it seemed a strong probability, even a virtual certainty, that India would remain committed to a peaceful, non-military nuclear policy, subject to the perfectly reasonable condition that Pakistan would not convert its nuclear option into weapons or explosions. This is where the positive element of conditional self-restraint operated in the post-1974 period.

ANALYSING VAJPAYEE'S DEFENCE

Let us, against the background of such a nuclear policy, look into the details of the official policy explanation for Pokhran-II. There are three key texts of explanation, all issuing from Vajpayee as Prime Minister. The first is his letter of May 11, 1998 to U.S. President Clinton. The second is his four-page *suo motu* statement of May 27, 1998 in Parliament, and the nine-page paper titled 'Evolution of India's Nuclear Policy' that goes with it. The third is his nine-page 'Statement Re: Bilateral Talks With United States,' made in the Rajya Sabha on December 15, 1998. Together they comprise the BJP-led regime's authoritative case for Pokhran-II and nuclear weaponization.

There are common points and overlapping arguments in these texts, but also some inconsistencies and contradictions. The most notable contradiction is between the more or less exclusive identification of China and Pakistan as security threats to India in the May 11 letter and the high-ground claim in the December 15 statement that India's concerns relating to disarmament and non-proliferation 'go beyond the South Asian region, and involve a wider perspective'. In the first text, not meant for public consumption, Vajpayee tries to win the U.S. President over to the idea of some sort of strategic anti-China convergence of interests. He cites Pakistan, the 'bitter neighbour', as the other leading element in 'the deteriorating security environment . . . faced by India for some years past'. But in the December 15 statement, which is meant to address political and public apprehensions about the content of the prolonged and secretive Indo–U.S. talks, the suggestion is that India has entered the nuclear weapons game as a global player, and not merely in response to the situation bordering India. This emphasis on the trans-regional and global nature of the concerns of Indian nuclear policy must also be understood to be in part a response to fears expressed around the world about the dangers of a nuclear confrontation between India and Pakistan and to the diplomatic pressure against nuclear weaponization brought to bear on the two countries, particularly by the Permanent Members of the United Nations Security Council (P-5), led by the United States.

The two parliamentary statements by the Prime Minister served different functions. The *suo motu* statement of May 27, along with the background paper dealing with the evolution of India's nuclear policy, represented the only serious defence of a pre-emptive and adventurist decision offered by the government. The December 15 statement, while defensive in approach and tone, was meant to be an update on India's nuclear policy in general and on the terms of the secret Indo–U.S. 'dialogue' in particular. It reflected the long distance travelled since the May 1998 explosions, the erosion of the independent element in India's nuclear policy, and the high-level decision to join the CTBT and the FMCT (when it is negotiated and ready) and accept other externally-imposed requirements of a 'nuclear restraint regime' while continuing with *de facto* weaponization.

The May 27 defence of Pokhran-II was based on the following core assertions and contentions:

The five May 1998 nuclear explosions are 'a continuation of the policies' set into motion that put India on 'the path of self-reliance and independence of thought and action'.

The 1980s and 1990s saw 'the gradual deterioration of our security environment' as a result of nuclear and missile proliferation. In addition, India has been 'the victim of externally aided and abetted terrorism, militancy and clandestine war'.

At a global level, the unequal and discriminatory regime of the NPT has been perpetuated and the nuclear weapons states have shown no willingness to 'take decisive and irreversible steps in moving towards a nuclear weapons-free world'.

Under these circumstances, the government faced a difficult decision and 'the touchstone that has guided us in making the correct choice clear was national security.'

India is now undeniably a nuclear weapons state. This status is 'not a conferment that we seek, nor is it a status for others to grant'. It is 'an endowment to the nation by our scientists and engineers'. It is also 'India's due, the right of one-sixth of humankind'.

India's nuclear weapons are 'weapons of self-defence,' which will ensure that the country is 'not subjected to nuclear threats or coercion.' The BJP-led government 'does not intend to engage in an arms race.'

India's nuclear policy has been marked by restraint and openness. 'Restraint, however, has to arise from strength. It cannot be based upon indecision or doubt.' The Pokhran-II explosions have led to the removal of doubts. The action involved has been 'balanced' in that 'it was the minimum necessary to maintain what is an irreducible component of our national security calculus'.

After displaying 'the assurance of action,' the government has announced

CTBT *Comprehensive Test Ban Treaty* FMCT *Fissile Material Cut-Off Treaty* NPT *Nuclear Non-Proliferation Treaty*

India's decision to observe 'a voluntary moratorium' and refrain from conducting underground nuclear test explosions. It has also signalled a willingness to 'move towards a *de jure* formalization of this declaration', thus meeting 'the basic obligation of the CTBT'. Further, the government has also indicated 'readiness to participate in negotiations in the Conference on Disarmament in Geneva on a Fissile Material Cut-off Treaty ' in 'the full confidence of the adequacy and credibility of the nation's weaponized nuclear deterrent'.

The Government of India will 'continue to be in the forefront' of the calls for opening negotiations for a Nuclear Weapons Convention along the lines of the Biological Weapons and Chemical Weapons conventions.

Disarmament continues to be 'a major plank' of the government's foreign policy.

The people of India, and Indians abroad, have 'with one voice spoken in favour of our action' and the government's nuclear policy is supported by an underlying consensus.

A close analysis shows the statement to be shot through with fallacies and inconsistencies.

The May 1998 Pokhran explosions represent a continuation of longstanding Indian nuclear policy in the same cynical Clausewitzian sense that war can be understood to be a continuation of policy by other means. India's nuclear policy with its twin components – the refusal to surrender nuclear sovereignty, and self-imposed and conditional restraint in not militarizing the option as part of the larger political commitment to global nuclear disarmament – was eminently sustainable. The accomplishment of the BJP-led government was to make a mockery of this longstanding policy by taking it towards the dishonourable goal of begging the discriminators for recognition as a minor player, a junior partner of the United States, in fact.

Vajpayee's reasoning, which claimed that national security was 'the touchstone that has guided us in making the correct choice', did not even attempt to show there was any change in the national security environment to warrant the adventurist decision to weaponize the nuclear option. His references to the 'gradual deterioration of our security environment' in the 1980s and 1990s and to India becoming a victim of 'externally aided and abetted terrorism, militancy and clandestine war' only substantiated the reading that the BJP came to the government with a pre-set agenda. It was the agenda of implementing the RSS–Bharatiya Jan Sangh–BJP vision of converting India into a chauvinistic-military power based on majoritarian rule and a Hindutva platform. The tirade against China, the references to Pakistan, and the hint of an anti-China strategic alliance between India and the United States in Vajpayee's leaked letter to Clinton further substantiated such a reading.

Read carefully, what Vajpayee's *suo motu* statement and the supporting policy paper reveal is that the BJP's nuclear game plan, if there was one, had virtually collapsed within two weeks of Pokhran-II. Instead, what the December 15, 1998 update revealed was, first, that among options the BJP-led government chose for itself in its effort to promote a 'nuclear restraint' regime in the sub-continent, the option of non-induction and non-deployment of nuclear weapons was absent. Secondly, the statement laid down for the first time before the Indian public broad contours of the nuclear defence posture, contours that were detailed earlier to the United States, the *de facto* mediator between India and Pakistan on the nuclear issue, in the Jaswant–Talbott talks. Thirdly, picking up a tendentious point developed by strategic affairs apologists for the hawkish course, the Prime Ministerial statement attempted a sleight-of-hand improvement of a plausible-sounding but tendentious claim made in the earlier statement. Whereas the claim on May 27 was that 'these tests are a continuation of *the policies* set into motion that put this country on the path of self-reliance and independence of thought and action'(emphasis added), the claim, clumsily worded, in the December 15 statement was a more reckless departure from the truth: 'The option that was exercised in May '98 was thus a continuation *of a decision* taken 25 years earlier . . . '(emphasis added). Thus, the false suggestion that India has had an unacknowledged nuclear weapons programme of long standing and that Pokhran-II was an inevitable sequel to the decision to stay out of the NPT, conduct a PNE in May 1974, and continue research and development relating to nuclear explosions.

Specifically, the update of December 15, 1998 indicated that the main features of the weaponizing nuclear policy were as follows.

India will deploy its nuclear deterrent: 'Just as our conventional defence capability has been deployed in order to safeguard the territorial integrity and sovereignty of India against any use or threat of use of force, the adoption of our nuclear deterrent posture has also followed the same

NPT *Nuclear Non-Proliferation Treaty* PNE *peaceful nuclear explosion/experiment* logic. . . . Ours will be a minimum credible deterrent, which will safeguard India's security – the security of one-sixth of humanity, now and into the future. The National Security Council, with the assistance of its subsidiary bodies . . . will make important contributions to elaborating these concepts'.

India's nuclear doctrine includes a policy of 'No-First-Use' and 'Non-Use against non-nuclear weapons states'.

A policy of 'No-First-Use' with a minimum nuclear deterrent 'implies deployment of assets in a manner that ensures survivability and capacity of an adequate response', in other words the development and deployment of a deterrent with a second-strike capability.

'India remains committed to converting our voluntary moratorium into a *de jure* obligation.' The Government of India is prepared to bring its discussions with 'key interlocutors' on 'a range of issues, including the CTBT' to a successful conclusion 'so that the entry into force of the CTBT is not delayed beyond September 1999'. Joining the CTBT will 'not constrain us from continuing with our R&D programmes, nor does it jeopardize in any manner the safety and effectiveness of our nuclear deterrent in the years to come'.

India is willing to join the FMCT negotiations in the Conference on Disarmament in Geneva and will be willing to work for the early conclusion of such a treaty, on the understanding that the treaty will be non-discriminatory. India will not agree to a moratorium on fissile material production pending the conclusion of an FMCT but will pay 'serious attention to any negotiated multilateral initiatives in the course of the FMCT negotiations'.

'In light of our additional capabilities, as a responsible state possessing nuclear weapons, and as earlier announced', India is taking steps to make its export control laws relating to 'sensitive technologies' more stringent. It also expects to be provided 'better access to dual-use and high technologies'.

India will continue its missile development programme, which is an 'indigenous programme' launched 15 years ago. Flight testing of an enhanced range Agni will proceed. The Government 'will not accept any restraints on the development of India's R&D capabilities' and 'remains unequivocally opposed to any suggestions that seek to place India at a technological disadvantage through intrusive or sovereignty-violative measures'.

It is evident from this discussion that the policy of nuclear weaponization imposed on the people of India by the BJP-led government represents not continuity, but a reactionary departure from

CTBT *Comprehensive Test Ban Treaty* FMCT *Fissile Material Cut-Off Treaty*

a well-conceived and tested policy with a balanced commitment to independence and peace. The course of inducting, stockpiling and deploying nuclear weapons and the pursuit of a 'minimum credible nuclear deterrent' and a second-strike capability must be recognized as nothing but a subversion of that policy.

5

SCIENCE, NUCLEAR CAPABILITIES AND THE BOMB

It is interesting that initially many of the political parties, notably the Congress(I), which later came out against the BJP's nuclear adventure, hailed the contribution made by the scientists involved. It was an integral part of the Vajpayee government's strategy of legitimization of its nuclear policy to portray Pokhran-II as a high point of Indian scientific achievement and to use the general public appreciation of Indian science and its successes to justify the departure from longstanding Indian nuclear policy. Prime Minister Vajpayee had declared in the Lok Sabha on May 27 that India's newly acquired 'nuclear weapons state' status was 'an endowment to the nation by our scientists and engineers'. Earlier, he announced that May 11 would be celebrated as National Technology Day; and added 'Jai Vigyan' ('Hail Science') to the slogan 'Jai Jawan, Jai Kisan' ('Hail Soldier, Hail Farmer'), coined in the days of the Indo–Pakistan conflict of 1965.[1]

SCIENTIFIC ACHIEVEMENTS IN PERSPECTIVE

The celebration of Indian science and technology that followed the five nuclear explosions necessitates placing achievements in the limited domain of nuclear weapons technology in a broader perspective.

How advanced is the weapons technology that Indian nuclear scientists have mastered? For a better idea of the scale of advanced technology involved, we can compare the reported achievements in nuclear testing to the degree of advance Indian nuclear scientists have made in the development of fast breeder reactors on a scale suitable for power generation. The Fast Breeder Test Reactor (FBTR) at Kalpakkam was generating power and was connected to the grid only in 1997, twelve years after it attained criticality.[2] Even that stage was reached several years behind schedule, with a good part of the delay blamed on the loss of the international collaboration with France. A full-scale power-producing fast breeder reactor is still on the drawing boards. Nuclear weapons technologies are, in several respects, simpler than those involved in peaceful uses like power generation. India's largely self-reliant performance in respect of power generation is noteworthy, yet lags considerably behind advanced western standards and has also not been able to deliver on the promises made.[3]

Nuclear weapons technology, it bears emphasis, is proven technology. The basic principles of its functioning and design are known and it has been established that these principles are correct. More than half a century after the deadly technology was developed, it is essentially a matter of procuring the fissile material and engineering design – and not of doing any deep, innovative science and technology. The Pokhran-II tests may have involved some new elements in this field or innovative ways of producing the fissile materials used, but none of these make the explosions an 'extraordinary' achievement. Interestingly, C.N.R. Rao, a chemist of international repute who has had a long involvement in decision-making in Indian science, described Pokhran-II as 'trivial science'.[4]

As early as 1967, the U.S. government conducted what came to be known as the 'Nth country experiment'. It was designed to see how much effort was actually required to develop a viable fission weapon design starting virtually from scratch. To quote Carey Sublette, author of the authoritative Internet resource, *Nuclear Weapons: Frequently Asked Questions*, on the details of the experiment: 'In this experiment, which ended on 10 April 1967, three newly graduated physics students were given the task of developing a detailed weapon design using only public domain information. The project reached a successful conclusion, that is, they did develop a viable design (detailed in the classified report UCRL-50248) after expending only three man-years of effort over two and a half calendar years. In the years since, much more information has entered the public domain, so that the level of effort required has obviously dropped further.'[5] Sublette's conclusion: 'This experiment established an upper limit on the required level of effort that is so low that the hope that lack of information may provide even a small degree of protection from proliferation is clearly a futile one.'

Freeman J. Dyson, well-known theoretical physicist, who has been closely associated with nuclear weapons and arms control issues and has frequently advised the U.S. government on these issues, points out that the basic principles of fission weapon design have been publicly available since 1964 and those of fusion weapon design since 1979. In his view, there is 'no longer any scientific glory attached to it. . . . Nobody with pretensions to be considered a serious scientist finds professional fulfillment in proving that he can design a bomb as competently as the Americans. Even in scientifically backward countries, young people of talent now know that nuclear weapons have ceased to be a scientific challenge'.[6]

However, much of nuclear weapons technology, which is old hat to serious scientists, remains a mystery and a secret to the lay public. This undoubtedly contributes something extra to the triumphalism that accompanies the acquisition and mastery of such technology. Such feelings are heightened by the frustration informed Indian public opinion has often expressed at the long record of U.S.-led sanctions against India's nuclear energy programme and the denial of access to other dual-use technology. This secrecy however is a double-edged weapon. It contributes to the ease with which the bogey of the competitor having stolen a march can be raised, a feature of nuclear weapons development well-known throughout the period of the Cold War. In India, major achievements and milestones in the development of indigenous capabilities in science and technology have always been greeted with enthusiasm. But in the case at hand, the abandoning of any sense of proportion in the celebration of India's mastery of advanced scientific knowledge points to an entirely different motivation – ultra-nationalism and jingoism. Indian science is seen to have established India as a nuclear weapons power, a 'global player' that cannot be ignored by the established nuclear weapons states.

As for the claims that the achievements of Indian scientists in Pokhran-II had delivered 'security' to the people of India, as nuclear scientists like Raja Ramanna declared, they were quickly shown to be exaggerated and dangerously short-sighted by Pakistan's nuclear tests, which came close on the heels of the Indian tests.[7] There is little doubt that Indian science and technology go deeper and are more sophisticated and broader in scope than anything that Pakistan can boast of. Nevertheless, Pakistan has clearly demonstrated a nuclear weapons capability. Chagai might not be able to match Pokhran-II's level of technical sophistication or demonstration of indigenous scientific capability. Nevertheless, the outcome is a destabilized security situation, an incipient nuclear arms race in the subcontinent. 'After our nuclear tests', asserted General Pervez Musharraf, Pakistan's Chief of Army Staff, 'Pakistan is talking to India on an equal basis. We are not talking to India from a weak position.'[8] An overblown estimation of the superiority of Indian science and technology in the two-week interregnum between Pokhran-II and Chagai appears to have blinded important sections of the BJP–RSS leadership to the virtual certainty that Pakistan would answer in kind. This failure of analysis prompted BJP–RSS stalwarts like Union Home Minister Lal Krishna Advani to make a provocative linkage between the Kashmir issue and self-proclaimed nuclear weapons status.

The notion that nuclear weapons will enhance security for India has been challenged on several counts by various commentators, including those with distinguished military experience like Admiral L. Ramdas, former Chief of the Indian Navy.[9] We will return to the issue of whether nuclear weapons can provide security and examine it in some detail.

THE SCIENTIFIC ESTABLISHMENT AND THE POLITICS OF THE BOMB

It is now clear that the contribution made by the atomic energy and defence research establishments to India's nuclear weaponization was by no means purely scientific or technical in nature. Over a period of many years, some senior scientists in these establishments played a pro-active role in building up pressure to conduct the tests. They thus provided important support to a political project of nuclear hawkishness.

DAE *Department of Atomic Energy* DRDO *Defence Research and Development Organization*

The evidence for this was originally indirect. It comprised mainly the strong public support for the government's decision to conduct the tests that came from the former leadership of the Indian nuclear energy establishment, in language that went well beyond any demands of scientific clarification. But important direct evidence was provided by the May 15, 1998, letter of former Prime Minister H. D. Deve Gowda to Prime Minister Vajpayee. It revealed that 'scientists had approached two previous governments to continue the tests, once in 1995 and then in 1997'; and that, like Narasimha Rao before him, 'I was requested to make a decision to conduct fresh nuclear tests. I convinced the scientists that the time was not ripe . . . .'[10]

Some senior DAE scientists, in public comments and in off-the-record statements to journalists, limited themselves to expressing their happiness that the Vajpayee government gave them the chance to demonstrate their capabilities and competence. It was one thing for DAE and DRDO scientists to do their best in their research programmes to fulfill the mandate given to them by the overall policy orientation. But claiming a right to extend the scientific part of the mandate to a point where it worked against the basic political tenets of Indian nuclear policy was to play an improper role in fuelling hawkishness and adventurism.

A striking example of the role of the nuclear establishment as a campaigner for weaponization in a volatile political context is provided by the remarks of the Chairman of the Atomic Energy Commission, R. Chidambaram, in an interview given to the Press Trust of India (PTI) on March 3, 1998.[11] This was when the probability of a BJP-led government was on everyone's mind. While nominally asserting that the final decision was political, he argued that nuclear tests were a necessity. In reply to a question whether the country could go nuclear as outlined in the manifesto of the BJP, he responded that 'the country was technologically ready and the capability was proved long back'. In the manner of a politician with a special interest in strategic affairs, the head of the nuclear establishment said that 'this preparedness itself was a testimony to the deterrent capability possessed by the country'. Asked whether the country could go ahead only with the help of simulations and by avoiding actual ground experiments, he retorted: 'Then what was the use of some countries going for 2000 explosions?' The report added: 'Speaking in favour of nuclear explosions to increase the data base for the country, he said computer simulations alone could not stand and [a] huge actual data base was required for simulations'. 'There was [a] huge difference between theoretical studies and practical experiments', he said, adding, 'if you are weak, people will try to take advantage of it'.

Along with the Deve Gowda testimony, this constitutes direct evidence that the DAE leadership went over to an active advocacy of testing and weaponization, building up a strong internal pressure to discard the earlier Indian policy line of conditional self-restraint on the nuclear option. It found in the ascent to power of a party committed to the chauvinistic vision of a Hindu Rashtra with nuclear teeth a congenial political turn, an opportunity not to be missed. .

BEHIND THE ARGUMENT OF NECESSITY

Let us now examine the nuclear scientist argument of 'necessity' for Pokhran-II. Strictly speaking, the argument relates not to 'scientific necessity' but to 'technological necessity'. Technological research of a particular kind becomes necessary insofar as the product or process sought to be developed or perfected is necessary. There is no argument to be made here, as there is in pure science, of the intrinsic value of all research. On the contrary, it is in the very nature of 'technologically necessary' nuclear weapons research that it raises the issues of annihilation and genocide.

Thus the question whether it was 'necessary' to conduct Pokhran-II is subsumed by the critical question of whether India needs nuclear weapons. Seen in this light, the public suggestion by the head of the nuclear energy establishment that nuclear tests were an overdue national necessity can be recognized not as a scientific, but as a loaded political statement.

In a context of a nuclear programme with proven nuclear weapon capabilities, where the nuclear option is kept open, non-testing may require scientists to take more innovative routes, of a theoretical or controlled laboratory nature, to validate their designs. If such a discipline is imposed by sober political decision-making in the interest of both peace and independence, then scientists must necessarily accept this course, even if the restraints are seen to stand in the way of further 'scientific–technological advance'. Chidambaram, while invok-

DAE *Department of Atomic Energy*

ing the argument of necessity, was aware that the existing technological level and preparedness kept India's nuclear option alive and active. That an untested nuclear option is a viable policy option is also demonstrated by the cases of South Africa and Israel. It has now been confirmed officially that the apartheid regime in South Africa had some half dozen nuclear weapons and that these 'bombs in the basement' were dismantled and destroyed, with the firm and clear-headed support of the African National Congress (ANC) and its leader, Nelson Mandela, in 1993.[12] It has long been known that Israel, with its policy of 'nuclear opacity', has had a formidable nuclear weapons capability – and a functional arsenal – even though it has thus far not conducted a single nuclear test.[13]

The pro-active stance on nuclear weapons testing of a small group of scientists in positions of importance and their increasingly open advocacy of the weaponization option must be recognized as a significant departure from the public style of the Indian scientific establishment. The sharp political emphasis and exaggerated language of the statements of scientific spokesmen in the immediate aftermath of Pokhran-II called attention to this departure. In a May 17, 1998 boast that has not been explained or elaborated subsequently, A.P.J. Abdul Kalam claimed on behalf of the DAE and the DRDO that with Pokhran-II the country had gained the capability to 'vacate' nuclear threats.[14] Such claims, as we have noted, are baseless. Chidambaram himself returned to his vision of a strong India in another interview immediately after the tests.[15] His reply to the question, 'Should we have nuclear weapons or keep the option open?' was:

> No comment. . . . The most important thing is that India must become strong. The greatest advantage of recognized strength is that you don't have to use it . . . everybody knows you are strong. Only when people see you as a weak country, they pressure you. We are a big country. We must learn to behave like a big country of one billion people. We should constantly remind ourselves of our strength.

Kalam did not lag behind. At his first press conference post-Pokhran, he broke off a technical exposition to remark on 'how a nuclear-armed India will be free of the fear of foreign invasions which have constantly remolded the ancient Hindu civilization'.[16] He added: 'For 2,500 years India has never invaded anybody. But others have come here, so many others have come'.

DRDO *Defence Research and Development Organization*

Thus, in the process of helping to overturn established nuclear policy and subsequently defending the new line, some top scientists have not merely provided support to the pursuit of the jingoistic agenda of a particular ideological–political formation. They have independently contributed to dangerous illusions of strength, invincibility and deterrence in the field of national defence and security as they interact with science. However, it must be noted that in subsequent months the tone of public comments by the scientific establishment in the atomic energy and defence research fields has been considerably more moderate. In part, this reflects the fact that with the progressive democratic campaign against nuclear weapons making political headway across India, the public debate has shifted increasingly from the scientific and technological aspects of the tests to the political and security implications of nuclear weaponization in the subcontinent. The swing in the BJP-led government's nuclear policy from vainglorious adventurism to virtual capitulation to the terms sought to be laid down by the United States and the discriminatory global nuclear order has also had a dampening influence on the attitudes of these top scientists. With the dangerous mess created in South Asia by the government of the Hindu Right staring people in the face, the euphoria over the wondrous 'endowment to the nation by our scientists and engineers' has vanished.

CURRENT INDIAN NUCLEAR CAPABILITIES

What precisely was achieved by the tests at Pokhran-II and what is the state of India's nuclear weapons capabilities from a scientific and technological standpoint? It is necessary to have a clear answer to this question for two reasons. First, the capabilities need to be measured against the key claims made by the BJP-led Government and the authorities of the DAE and the DRDO. The claims are that India has obtained the data it requires from the Pokhran-II tests, that no further tests are necessary from a scientific and technological angle, and that India is now ready for the CTBT with a 'proven' nuclear weapons programme in place. Secondly, the possible operational meaning of the assertion that India will deploy a 'minimal credible nuclear deterrent' and its implications for peace, security and stability in the South Asian and global context can be assessed only if we

DAE *Department of Atomic Energy* DRDO *Defence Research and Development Organization* have a scientifically dependable answer to the question of current capabilities.

TESTING NUCLEAR WEAPONS

Before we attempt to answer this question, we need to review some basic facts about nuclear weapons and testing that have been important to the CTBT debate.[17] Among the different classes of nuclear weapons, there is a clear hierarchy with regard to the amount of explosive testing needed to develop weapons of each class.

Highly enriched uranium weapons with a gun-barrel type assembly require the least amount of testing. In these weapons, the uranium is kept divided and brought together when the explosion is to be initiated by firing the separate pieces at each other using ordinary explosives (of the type used in artillery shells). The bomb used on Hiroshima was of this type and the design had not been tested previously.

Although fission weapons with plutonium can, in principle, be produced without testing, in practice they are tested. In the case of plutonium weapons, the fissile material is present in one piece but at its normal density. The fissile material has then to be compressed to much higher densities in a few microseconds (one microsecond = 1/1,000,000 of a second) using special high explosives. This is known as the implosion method. The weapon used over Nagasaki was of this type; such a weapon had previously been tested at the so-called Trinity test, the first nuclear weapon explosion to be conducted.

Boosted fission weapons need more testing than ordinary fission weapons. In this type of fission weapons, the efficiency of the chain reaction is enhanced ('boosted') by increasing the number of neutrons available utilizing neutrons produced by the fusion process. A few grams of deuterium and tritium are introduced in gaseous form in the core of the fissile material for this purpose. Since the tritium decays due to its own radioactivity, the gas has to be replaced after some years.

True thermonuclear weapons, as we have mentioned earlier, are two stage weapons. The first stage, referred to as the primary stage, is a fission device or a boosted fission device. The radiation from this explosion compresses the 'secondary' charge of deuterium, usually

CTBT *Comprehensive Test Ban Treaty*

used in solid form as the chemical lithium deuteride. The main fusion reaction is again from the fusion of deuterium and tritium, where the tritium is produced *in situ* by neutrons colliding with the lithium (actually lithium-6), leading to the explosion of the 'secondary' stage. Such weapons can be built to give virtually unlimited yield. There will be very little confidence in such weapons without explosive testing.

What can be learned, broadly speaking, from the different types of tests of nuclear weapons?

Explosive testing of nuclear weapons has played a major role in validating the design of nuclear weapons, obtaining data for their improvement, and for fresh designs. The number of tests done by each nuclear weapons state for a new weapon design has varied, ranging from an average of six for the U.S. to a reported 22 in the case of France.

The basic reason for this is that while the fundamental physics laws that govern the behaviour of nuclear weapons are well-known, actual weapon performance involves a lot of detail that cannot be worked out completely from first principles. An important example is the detailed behaviour and properties of the fissile material mass in the extreme conditions of pressure and temperature that prevail as the nuclear chain reaction proceeds leading to the explosion. These can be approximated and modelled partially by computer, but in general, such results have to be compared with experiments. Fewer tests can be used to validate such nuclear weapons codes, but the corresponding weapons design will have much less flexibility.

Explosive tests that allow the fission chain reaction to proceed without hindrance to the release of nuclear energy are prohibited under the CTBT; this is the so-called zero-yield barrier. The ban does not rule out what are known as Sub-Critical Experiments (SCEs). One form of SCEs is when high pressure can be put on a plutonium mass by hitting it with an aluminium plate driven by a high-explosive charge. Such 'equation of state' tests provide information on the state of the fissile material for some ranges of pressure and temperature. There is no danger of criticality (that is, a very low-yield nuclear explosion) in such a situation.

There are also other SCEs that can be done, particularly to study the effect of the high explosive on the core of fissile material, a subject

CTBT *Comprehensive Test Ban Treaty*

important to weapons design. Such experiments, when conducted with the fissile material replaced by inert material (which will nevertheless be radioactive and toxic), are referred to as 'hydrotests'. The term SCEs generally refers to the actual use of fissile material, in which it has to be carefully ensured that over-criticality is not achieved. Over-criticality is a particular risk with plutonium weapons because plutonium behaves in a complex manner under extreme conditions. These require underground testing facilities.

In the case of boosted fission weapons or the boosted fission primary stage of a two-stage thermonuclear device, the mixing of the boost gas with the plutonium under the impact of the high-explosive is an important issue that is studied by sub-critical tests. There appears to be no real analogue of SCEs for the secondary fusion stage of thermonuclear weapons.

Another class of tests not permitted under the CTBT is the 'hydronuclear test'. Here, slight over-criticality is achieved; in other words, there is the actual release of nuclear energy (typically, the equivalent of a few kg yield).

These tests have been important in understanding the behaviour of nuclear weapons to ensure that they are safe from accidental detonation. The U.S. standard here is referred to as 'one-point' safety, that is, ensuring that there is only a slight release of nuclear energy in case the high explosive is accidentally detonated at one point (by a rifle bullet, for instance). More than 40 such tests were conducted by the U.S. early in its programme (1958–61). They are no longer deemed necessary. Such tests for safety are particularly important for ready-to-use nuclear warheads for missiles and artillery shells and for boosted fission weapons where the fissile material cannot be kept separated from the weapon.

Apart from some of the tests described here, there is a large class of non-explosive tests done on the various components that make up the nuclear weapon.

After this review of basic facts about nuclear weapons testing, let us sum up the official version of what was done at Pokhran.[18] Five nuclear underground explosions of different types and yields were conducted over two days at the Pokhran test range. On May 11, three devices were detonated simultaneously. One was a fission weapon with a claimed yield of 15 kilotons (kt), the second a thermonuclear

SCE *Sub-Critical Experiment* CTBT *Comprehensive Test Ban Treaty* device with a claimed yield of 45 kt, and the third a sub-kiloton device with a yield of 0.2 kt. On May 13, two devices were detonated simultaneously, with claimed yields of 0.5 kt and 0.3 kt. It was later made clear that the purpose of the sub-kiloton tests was to validate the one- and two-dimensional neutronic and hydrodynamic weapons codes.[19] It was also stated that the Bhabha Atomic Research Centre (BARC) had worked for more than 25 years on the design and development of different varieties of nuclear explosives and related technologies, such as improving the shelf life of device components and maximizing the yield-to-weight ratio.

Subsequently, a senior DAE scientist, S.K. Sikka, stated on record that the primary of the thermonuclear device was a boosted fission device.[20] Reliable internal sources also indicate that the DAE has acquired the ability to conduct 'equation-of-state' tests by hitting plutonium targets with high-explosive-driven projectiles, using X-ray probes to study the behaviour of plutonium under these conditions.

From the beginning, the total yield of the May 11 explosions has been the subject of controversy. The main challenge has come from seismologists in the United States; their estimates of the total yield of the May 11 tests are significantly lower than the DAE's claims. The Indian nuclear establishment's contention that the American seismologists have not taken into account the simultaneous nature of the explosions, which would have led them to make a lower estimate, was challenged by B.K. Subba Rao.[21] The controversy is yet to be satisfactorily settled; it clearly awaits an independent and unbiased scientific analysis of the conflicting claims and an independent analysis of the seismic data.[22]

Another feature of the official claims has been the lack of clarity about why simultaneous explosions were conducted, despite the fact that that particular feature of the tests has been presented as a scientific achievement. The former Chairman of the Atomic Energy Regulatory Board, A. Gopalakrishnan, has been sharply critical of this choice; he has pointed out that scientifically speaking, simultaneous tests would not help in validating weapons codes and that separate tests would have served the purpose better.[23] In his view, this choice has been dictated by the political consideration of minimizing international pressure on the Government of India rather than any scientific or technological rationale.

DAE *Department of Atomic Energy*

Let us assume for the purpose of the discussion that follows that official Indian claims about the yield and nature of their weapons are basically correct. Summarizing the official information, most of the Pokhran-II devices were clearly plutonium-based implosion weapons. There was a single test of a thermonuclear device in an unknown configuration. There were clearly no tests in the hydronuclear range of yield (again on the presumption that the data on yields are correct).

From the earlier discussion on the types and extent of testing for various classes of nuclear weapons and the official version of Pokhran-II, we can now arrive at the following assessment of the capabilities of the Indian nuclear programme.

First, it is clear that no reliable thermonuclear weapon can be built, particularly for deployment as missile warheads. Whatever the code used to design the thermonuclear device claimed to have been tested at Pokhran, it has most probably been insufficiently validated. Second, as with the thermonuclear weapon, the boosted fission weapon configurations have most probably not been adequately validated. The fact that the boosted fission device tested was part of a thermonuclear device would have made it more difficult to obtain data to validate the functioning of an independent boosted fission weapon. Third, it appears that the only reasonably validated nuclear weapon was an implosion-type plutonium device. It is not clear whether this has provided the nuclear energy establishment the flexibility to design tactical nuclear weapons. It is also unclear how much flexibility there will be, even for fission weapons, in terms of weapons design with the most advanced characteristics.

Fourth, given the fact that no hydronuclear tests were conducted, important questions remain about the reliability and safety – to the user – of such weapons. The one- and two-dimensional weapons codes developed and tested do not adequately answer the demands of safety, which calls for three-dimensional codes. Questions of safety are important for fully armed nuclear warheads, especially if they are mounted on delivery systems. No attention seems to have been paid to the issue of safety in the DAE authorities' comments on the weapons tests, although it has dominated the CTBT debate, especially in the United States.

Regarding the ability to undertake SCEs, only one of the range

CTBT *Comprehensive Test Ban Treaty* SCE *Sub-Critical Experiment* of techniques that the term encompasses appears to be currently available to India. But even if more advanced techniques of sub-critical testing are developed, they will be insufficient to validate designs of either thermonuclear weapons or boosted fission weapons, especially given the fact that only a single combined test of the two types has been claimed. It is also important to ensure that sub-critical tests with plutonium do not 'creep up' to the hydronuclear range; this too will be difficult to ensure without further testing.[24]

As for claims of computer simulation capabilities, the issue is not really the availability of super-computing power. The utility of super-computing capabilities lies in two aspects of weapons design in a non-explosive testing regime. One is the challenge of calculating the behaviour of nuclear weapons in detail from the basic physics principles with as little empirical input as possible. The second is the challenge of extending empirical codes to study more complicated weapons configurations, or even fresh ones, using the input from sub-critical tests as well as tests with inert material. However, such exercises are not of much use when there is little data to validate the final computer codes developed. It is not possible to design weapons by calculations based on basic physics principles alone, especially for the fusion stage of thermonuclear devices.

Persistence with nuclear weaponization under these conditions is highly unstable; the situation could eventually lead to a demand for fresh testing of a wide range of devices. Speaking at a seminar in New Delhi, K. Santhanam, the head of the DRDO, observed that the weapon designers would certainly like to conduct more tests if that were possible.[25] He added that this could not be done without a political decision in the matter. Summarizing the results of Pokhran-II, he said that a 'thermonuclear device' was tested along with a 'fission device, which was a warhead'. Quite clearly, thermonuclear weapons capability has not been established by India's nuclear energy establishment.

In short, current capabilities amount to only moderately reliable, safety-untested weapons of the plutonium-based implosion type without too much leeway in the choice of delivery systems. Quite apart from the problems associated with the design of a suitable command, control, communications and intelligence (C^3I) system, such capability hardly merits the description of a 'minimum credible nuclear

DRDO *Defence Research and Development Organization*

deterrent', even if we assume for the sake of the technical argument that deterrence theory is valid.

Thus there can be no doubt that, scientifically speaking, the claims made by authorities of the DAE and the DRDO at the press conference of May 17, 1998 to the effect that the five nuclear explosions provided 'critical data for the validation of our capability in the design of nuclear weapons of different yields for different applications and different delivery systems' and that they 'have significantly enhanced our capability in computer simulation of new designs and taken us to the stage of sub-critical experiments in the future, if considered necessary' are seriously exaggerated.[26]

In the context of the CTBT, Chidambaram has claimed that the Pokhran-II tests have contributed enough data to enable the validation of three basic weapon designs.[27] Apart from reiterating the claims of thermonuclear and fission weapon capabilities, he has claimed that the sub-kiloton device can be used as a tactical nuclear weapon, the first explicit statement by a DAE or DRDO official to this effect. In Chidambaram's opinion, 'After one test in 1974 we could not have signed the CTBT but today after five sophisticated . . . modern nuclear tests we can go ahead and sign'. Further, claiming that modern developments have rendered a few tests in 1998 equal to several in the past, he asserts: 'We have enough data and we don't need to test again.' Interestingly, the claim to tactical nuclear and thermonuclear weapons capability has been implicitly challenged by Chidambaram's predecessor as Chairman of the AEC, P. K. Iyengar. Doubts that the five tests could have given India a 'minimum credible nuclear deterrent' have also been expressed by other commentators, including pro-weaponization ones.[28]

The DAE claims were reiterated by Chidambaram in an interview to *Frontline*: 'So if in 1998 India had carried out the tests based on today's knowledge of physics, engineering, material science and electronics, there is a kind of leapfrogging here, and each one of the tests should be considered equivalent to several tests carried out by other nuclear weapons states'.[29] In a general sense, this statement sounds plausible, but what is clear is that there are several aspects of weapons design that simply cannot be completed without adequate testing. The stance that fewer tests are needed today than they were several years ago to attain a 'credible nuclear deterrent' does not ap-

DAE *Department of Atomic Energy* CTBT *Comprehensive Test Ban Treaty* AEC *Atomic Energy Commission*

pear to be borne out by the information available on the nuclear weapons programmes of other countries (see box). As for the current official Indian claims to thermonuclear power status, they are unlikely to carry any weight in international expert circles.

It should be obvious that our analysis is not intended to bolster the case for further testing, least of all for the purpose of establishing or improving weapons designs. On the contrary, it explores the scientific and technological dimension of the nuclear misadventure. It shows that the rationale advanced by the proponents of nuclear weaponization for joining the CTBT after Pokhran-II is based, on the one hand, on the subversion of a well-tested policy committed to independence as well as peace and, on the other, on exaggerated claims that collapse under any serious scientific scrutiny.

To complete the picture of Indian nuclear weapons capabilities, we need to look beyond the warheads. A deployable nuclear deterrent requires more than explosive devices. To be operational, it requires delivery systems and C^3I systems. India's current delivery system capabilities are quite limited. Two components of a triad, namely strike aircraft and land-based missiles, could conceivably be put to-

EXPLOSIVE TESTS AND THERMONUCLEAR WEAPONS

What does the Stockpile Stewardship and Management Plan (SSMP), the basic blueprint for the management of the United States nuclear arsenal under the CTBT regime, have to say about the role of explosive tests in validating thermonuclear weapon designs? The document, the February 1996 version of which was declassified by the U.S. government due to pressure from environmental groups, states in Section IV-27:*

> However, the high energy-density conditions relevant to secondary performance are extremely difficult to create in a laboratory setting and most data must be extrapolated to the weapons regime in at least some parameters, requiring the expert judgement of weapons scientists following a careful strategy of fundamental science, scaled experiments, and comparison with past nuclear test data to validate models. Laser and pulsed power experiments, as well as computer and simulation modelling advances, are critical to obtaining fundamental physics data that when validated with past nuclear test data, can be used to assess the full nuclear performance of the secondary stage.

Technicalities apart, the bottom line is clear: past nuclear test data are essential for the development of thermonuclear weapons. Even if a projected Indian thermonuclear weapon capability is going to be far less flexible and far less sophisticated than the U.S. version, the claim that one test is sufficient for validating a

CTBT *Comprehensive Test Ban Treaty*

reliable thermonuclear weapons code lacks credibility.

With respect to boosted-fission weapons, the SSMP states in Section IV-26:

> The other key technical issues associated with primaries involve the ignition and burn of their boost gas, which are extremely difficult to access experimentally without nuclear testing. Laser and other inertial confinement fusion approaches, and pulsed power experiments may be able to provide an improved understanding of the aspects [*sic*] of gas burn physics. The data gathered in this complete set of experiments will be essential for evaluating new and evolving computational models of the primary stage behavior.

In other words, boosted-fission weapons development also depends crucially on explosive test data. The crux of the matter in both cases is that when it comes to the fusion part, starting from just the basic rules and building the entire weapons code in a reliable way is virtually impossible. A good part of the investment in fundamental physics under the SSMP is to see if reliance on explosive test data can be reduced.

According to experts, new fundamental physics developments do not automatically lead to better weapons codes.

Recent advances in the understanding, from a fundamental physics viewpoint, of some physical parameters in fusion processes led to a more consistent interpretation of astrophysical data on stellar behaviour. When these advances were incorporated into weapons codes, the results of the codes did not match the data of the previous thermonuclear tests. This is discussed in a publication of the U.S.-based National Resources Defence Council titled *Explosive Alliances: Nuclear Weapons Research at American Universities*, by Thomas B. Cochran and Christopher E. Paine (NRDC publication, January 1998). Indeed, the authors fear that fundamental physics research related to nuclear weapons may lead to fresh demands for explosive testing even in the advanced U.S. context The implication for India is obvious. Better fundamental physics or technical understanding at the theoretical level alone is not enough. Thermonuclear weapons development will inevitably lead to hawkish demands for resuming explosive testing.

*Note: The sanitised version of the SSMP is available in *End Run.*

gether; submarine-based missiles are not on the short-term agenda.

The first component, perhaps the simplest in the triad, is probably quite undeveloped, with no clear choice made yet of the aircraft to be used to carry the nuclear warheads.[30] Even these would require modification before anything more complex than simple 'free fall' bombs can be contemplated. Delivery by strike aircraft is not, in any case, a serious option beyond the immediate Indian neighbourhood.

The second option would require the development of a missile capability considerably more advanced than what is available today. A key element in this is the development of the extended range ver-

SSMP *Stockpile Stewardship Management Plan*

sion of the Agni missile, which has two stages, both of which use solid propellants. Despite the claims of Defence Minister Fernandes that the test firing has taken India to 'the point of operationalization of Agni II as a weapons system', it appeared that there was still some way to go from such tests to the development of missiles with adequate payload capacity and suitably designed warheads. As we have already noted, an Indian nuclear weapons programme is likely to have little flexibility in warhead design, as a result of the limited testing undertaken.

Command and control systems for nuclear weapons will also take considerable time to develop before anything reasonably sophisticated, meeting the military requirements springing from the proximity of India and Pakistan, gets in place.

How credible then is India's 'nuclear deterrent' in the light of this scientific assessment of its nuclear weapons, delivery systems and command and control capabilities after Pokhran-II? Clearly the capabilities pose little challenge to the dominance of the nuclear weapons powers, particularly the United States, and the asymmetry between India's capabilities and those of the P-5 will remain essentially unaltered. In fact, India's current nuclear status is probably best described as 'pseudo-weaponized' and it is extremely unlikely that its 'nuclear deterrent' will become 'credible' in any global sense in the foreseeable future. Inflating the scientific and technological outcome of Pokhran-II to justify signing the CTBT must be recognized as a cynical attempt to retain a posture of weaponization at any cost.

However, Indian capabilities in relation to Pakistan are an entirely different matter: they are sufficient to threaten this neighbour. In turn, Pakistan will almost certainly be able to deploy, even if at a considerable economic and social cost, a nuclear force sufficient to threaten India. It is in the South Asian context that continued weaponization by India and Pakistan creates a dangerously unstable situation. Given the physical proximity of the two countries, their history of armed conflicts, incidents and tensions, and the presence of jingoistic political–ideological elements in the government and polity of both countries, nuclear weaponization programmes even at the rather undeveloped level described in this section pose a grave threat to the safety and security of the peoples of the subcontinent. It is to these issues that we turn next.

CTBT *Comprehensive Test Ban Treaty*

6

NUCLEAR WEAPONS AND SECURITY IN SOUTH ASIA

The security rationale for India's nuclear weapons as argued by the pro-weaponization lobby has always been character ized by a certain ambiguity. At times, overt weaponization has been justified as a necessary insurance against nuclear blackmail by the P-5, with China's nuclear weapons build-up and U.S. sabre-rattling during the 1971 Bangladesh conflict leading the list of specific examples in support of this argument. On other occasions, the alleged nuclear threat posed by a hostile Pakistan or, more accurately, Pakistan's nuclear capability, has been offered as the rationale. This is reflected especially in statements meant for domestic consumption.

Elements of both arguments characterized the rhetoric of the BJP-led government in the immediate run-up to Pokhran-II and also in its aftermath. The December 15, 1998 authoritative defence of policy reversal by the Prime Minister confined itself to the bare assertion that the nuclear deterrent posture followed the same logic as that of India's conventional defence capability, namely, 'to safeguard the territorial integrity and sovereignty of India against any use or threat of use of force'.[1] Noting that regional issues had been kept apart from disarmament and non-proliferation in the Jaswant–Talbott talks, the statement asserted that 'India's concerns in these matters go beyond the South Asian region, and involve a wider perspective'. The suggestion, then, is that India has entered the nuclear weapons game as a global player, not merely in response to regional compulsions.

It is therefore essential to examine whether the pursuit of nuclear weaponization is sustainable in the South Asian context. Underpinning the defence of nuclear weaponization in the subcontinent is the argument that while nuclear weapons are necessary for global security reasons, nuclear deterrence will in fact ensure stability and security in terms of the subcontinental situation, provided matters are handled suitably with Pakistan and China. India's nuclear doctrines are to be developed with this basic argument in mind.

It is not very difficult to see that such reasoning is untenable. In any realistic assessment, there is nothing in the announced nuclear postures that guarantees security or stability. An arms race is inevitable and India will lose substantially rather than gain from the current path of weaponization.

Let us recall in summary the nuclear defence posture outlined by Prime Minister Vajpayee in his Rajya Sabha statement of December 15, 1998. First, India was to have a 'minimum credible deterrent'. Secondly, this nuclear deterrent would be deployed. Thirdly, the new nuclear doctrine would include a policy of 'no-first-use' and also non-use of nuclear weapons against non-nuclear weapons states. Fourthly, as a corollary to the no-first-use policy, the aim was to achieve a 'deployment of assets that ensures survivability and capacity of an adequate response', in other words, a second-strike capability.

It is well known that Pakistan has long considered its nuclear weapons capability not merely as a tit-for-tat answer to India's, but also as a hedge against India's strategic superiority in conventional arms. Interestingly, in a colourful statement made on the floor of the U.S. Senate in November 1981, Senator Daniel Patrick Moynihan, ex-Ambassador to India, underlined the same point with reference to Pokhran-I.[2] Before Pokhran-II, Pakistan had even rejected a suggestion that it sign with India a pact on no-first-use of nuclear capabilities. In the light of this, it was predictable that Pakistan would not join India in a no-first-use pact but instead propose a general reduction of arms on both sides, linking conventional arms to nuclear weapons. By its acceptance of the logic of deterrence, the current Indian nuclear defence posture serves to validate Pakistan's position.

In this context, no-first-use can be described as a stance that reduces nuclear tensions only partially. While it is better than the nuclear defence postures of the P-5 barring China (a fact that domestic apologists of weaponization do not tire of reminding us), it makes clear that nuclear weapons will be inducted and deployed by India. This provides Pakistan an opportunity to claim that it needs the capability to match India's weapons, thus creating conditions for an India-Pakistan nuclear standoff.

Indeed, this is the same logic by which both the BJP and strategic affairs experts have often argued for an Indian nuclear deterrent to match Chinese capabilities.[3] What is sauce for the Indian goose can justifiably be sauce for the Pakistani gander.

THE LOGIC OF A NUCLEAR ARMS RACE

Under such circumstances, an arms race is inevitable. If India's stance would be one of pushing to protect its nuclear weapons and delivery systems in order to maintain a credible second-strike capability, then Pakistan's would logically be the stance of trying to override this advantage by developing a substantially greater first-strike capability. If a policy of deterrence is indeed what the two countries are going to follow, then the pious statements from the governments of India and Pakistan that they do not want an arms race can be entirely discounted. Given the relatively backward technological infrastructure and capabilities and the general economic conditions of the two countries, however, the policy will be implemented not at the breathless pace of weaponization seen at the height of the Cold War but in a slow-motion replay of it.

It would be futile and counter-productive for India to try and win such a race by virtue of its greater economic strength. In the context of nuclear weaponization, a weakened, rather than stable, Pakistan is likely to pose a greater concern for India's security (it must be added, for the sake of even-handedness, that from a Pakistani standpoint, a weakened, rather than stable, India is likely to be a greater concern to Pakistan's security). The proponents of nuclear weaponization have apparently not paid any attention to a lesson that can be learnt from Russia's experience: faced with a deterioration of its conventional military strength over the past few crisis-ridden years, Russia has resiled from its commitment to no-first-use of nuclear weapons and the Russian Duma has seriously resisted the ratification of START-II.

The clarifications given to the Rajya Sabha by the Prime Minister and the External Affairs Minister on the term 'minimum' in India's minimum credible deterrent hardly helped matters.[4] According to these clarifications, the 'minimum' is not to be understood as a definite number or to be pinned down in any way, but is to remain flexible, to be decided as the security situation warrants, or, in plain-speak, to be decided unilaterally by India as the government of the day deems fit. Such a posture is obviously not conducive to avoiding an arms race or developing a 'nuclear restraint' regime in tandem with Pakistan since it leaves unclear what India seeks to build by way of a nuclear arsenal. What is minimal for Indian security hawks with respect to China will certainly not be seen as minimal by Pakistan.

Further specific implications of nuclear weaponization depend on the assessment of the current capabilities of India and Pakistan. We have already examined India's current capabilities at some length. Pakistan indisputably possesses the capability for highly enriched uranium weapons, possibly with sufficient flexibility to deliver them as missile warheads. The fission weapons that both countries possess will initially be deliverable only by aircraft, but one may reasonably expect that warheads deliverable by short-range missiles will be available in the near term. Densely populated areas in both India and Pakistan will be within the range of nuclear weapons. In the medium term, the development of longer-range missiles will render even larger parts of the two countries vulnerable to attack. Submarine-based missiles, an extremely costly proposition, appear to be a long way off, if they are going to be inducted at all. C^3I systems on both sides will take considerable time to develop.

The adventurist test-launch of Agni II, and the Pakistani answer to it, amount to forcing the pace of the South Asian arms race and destabilizing whatever temporary equation seemed to be established after the nuclear explosions of May 1998. The destabilization of security calculations built into the pursuit of deterrence seemed at work. The aggressive Indian official boasts invited retaliatory claims from Pakistani government and Army leaders about nuclear, missile and superior fighting capabilities. General Pervez Musharraf, Pakistan's Chief of Army Staff, was quoted as saying : 'We have reached a cer-

START *Strategic Arms Reduction treaties*

tain level within our means and to maintain or enhance that level would not cost much.... our problem is not of reaching anywhere in the world. Let them spend the money on building Agnis.... We have the capability of reaching anywhere in India and will destroy a few cities, if required'. 'In order to deal with the threat mainly from India', he claimed, the Pakistan Joint Staff Headquarters had calculated a force level adequate to 'deter aggression'; and the Pakistan armed forces had the capability of 'ending the war on a favourable note'. Significantly, following the provocation of the Agni II test launch, Pakistan's Chief of Army Staff elaborated on plans for a C^3I system which he claimed would be in place by mid-May 1999.[5] One could not have asked for a quicker and more convincing debunking of the claim that nuclear weaponization would not lead to an arms race and increase tensions in the subcontinent.

In sum, India's nuclear capabilities will not bring it anywhere close to the league of the existing nuclear weapons states and therefore its 'minimum credible nuclear deterrent' will not be taken seriously even within the framework of deterrence theory as it exists. That the government of the Hindu Right and the pro-weaponization lobbies in India were quite aware of this unflattering reality was clear from the unctuousness with which the government initiated a series of security dialogues with the nuclear weapons states, with the sole and significant exception of China. What is plain to any informed external observer is that India's standoff in nuclear weaponry will be exclusively with Pakistan. The current suggestion of a global security rationale, which was absent in the perspective presented by Vajpayee's letter to Clinton, represents a defensive response to fears expressed worldwide about the dangers of a nuclear confrontation in the subcontinent and to the political–diplomatic pressure brought to bear on India and Pakistan, particularly by the P-5 led by the United States.

It is unlikely that India's claimed second-strike capability will be put to any serious test at the present stage. Currently, if India's missiles and nuclear-capable aircraft are not deployed near the border, they are likely to be invulnerable. Neither Pakistan's delivery systems nor its C^3I capabilities will enable it to target these assets so effectively as to incapacitate them in their entirety. Conversely, any forward deployment of these assets to sites closer to the border will be read as an aggressive gesture. Such adventurism is likely to promote an increased state of readiness of Pakistan's nuclear arsenal. India's linkage of missiles to nuclear warheads, made explicitly in several statements after Pokhran-II, has rendered the forward deployment of its short-range missiles as a conventional deterrent problematic. In general, the continued development of missiles and suitable warheads can be expected to be a destabilizing factor since they are harder to detect and less vulnerable to interception and have much shorter flight times (of the order of a few minutes) than strike aircraft. A cheaper second-strike option, such as one involving short-range nuclear-tipped missiles on mobile launchers, can add substantially to instability in crisis conditions and encourage Pakistan to use a similar strategy. Defence Minister Fernandes has confirmed that this is indeed the intended strategy of the government in his remarks after the test-launch of the Agni II.[6]

For the next several years, potential Indian and Pakistani nuclear arsenals are unlikely to possess the ability to incapacitate or seriously damage each other's military, particularly nuclear, assets. Each side will be far more capable of seriously damaging the other's civilian targets. Pakistan can, with a fair degree of certainty, inflict serious damage on at least a few major Indian population centres and India can certainly react in like manner. But is it credible that an Indian government will be willing to gamble with the lives of millions of people and not actually shift to a first-strike posture in a crisis situation? No-first-use may be an announced doctrine. But if there is a grave crisis with the possibility of a nuclear confrontation, the temptation to move towards a first-strike posture will be overwhelming if nuclear weapons are already deployed. Armies in the real world plan for the use – not the non-use – of their weapons.

The proponents of weaponization argue that since India is a peace-loving country that has never initiated an attack on a neighbouring country, Pakistan should accept India's mutual no-first-use offer. But the development of a regime of nuclear restraint on this basis requires that the other side accept the argument even under extreme conditions. Such moral claims, sharply disputed already, will tend to be even less acceptable to the other side now that India has declared itself a nuclear weapons state, seeks to deploy a nuclear arsenal, and speaks about developing a second-strike capability. If such arguments are genuinely meant, it would then appear that the government of the Hindu Right, egged on by the pro-weaponization lobby, has pushed the country towards nuclear weaponization by compromising its security in the near term and exposing its population to a first-strike capability in the event of a crisis, all in exchange for an illusory insurance against possible nuclear threats in the distant future from unidentified sources.

Even if, for the sake of argument, we accept the terms of deterrence theory, stability in the subcontinent with fully deployed nuclear weapons will depend critically on the ability of India and Pakistan to read and influence the thinking of the other in relation to its security, and also to be able to understand the possible reactions of the other in various situations. The two sides need to communicate to each other through words and deeds. Deterrence theory holds that to be successful this requires, apart from constant political–diplomatic communication that will be at a premium in India–Pakistan crisis situations, substantial technical investment in C^3I. Sophisticated and expensive C^3I would appear to be a necessity even if India and Pakistan do not use the high-alert, counterforce strategies of the United States and the Soviet Union during the Cold War. With deployed weapons but without sophisticated C^3I systems in place, wrong signals or the misreading of each other's intentions and capabilities are bound to heighten the danger of actual use of nuclear weapons.

Accidental use of nuclear weapons is also a real danger to be guarded against. As Pervez Hoodbhoy, the well-known Pakistani physicist and anti-nuclear weapons activist, has pointed out, if weaponization is not rolled back through democratic and popular pressure, Pakistan and India, given their low C^3I capabilities, are likely to opt for a dispersed deployment of nuclear weapons.[7] With such an option, the natural strategy will be to promote the decision-making autonomy of nuclear-armed units. This is bound to multiply the dangers of unauthorized or accidental use of nuclear weapons. Nor is it clear that any C^3I system will be able to cope with the kind of problems that arise from the geographical proximity of India and Pakistan, including flight times for missiles that will be of the order of a few minutes. The margin available for determining whether an alarm is genuine or false will be extremely small.

The troubled record of India-Pakistan relations bristles with instances of border 'incidents' and confrontations, major as well as minor, that would be deadly in a nuclear-armed environment. Without independent intelligence capability, including national technical means such as satellites, both sides are also vulnerable to misapprehensions and misinformation from third parties. The development of appropriate C^3I capabilities is, in fact, a long process; the situation in the intervening period is likely to be volatile. We have already cited (see Chapter 3) expert testimony that during the Cold War the United States and the Soviet Union, especially the former, often failed to read the other's words and deeds correctly despite high-quality C^3I capabilities, and that this led to incredibly critical situations. There is no reason whatever to believe that an India–Pakistan nuclear standoff will be an exception to this rule.

Overall, it appears that after Pokhran-II and Chagai, India's nuclear policy and nuclear defence posture have succeeded only in degrading, if not compromising, the country's security. It is clearer now than it ever was that the longstanding policy of keeping the nuclear option open on the basis of self-restraint, opposition to the discriminatory global nuclear order, and a serious commitment to nuclear disarmament was eminently sustainable. In fact, it can be recognized as the only policy that could have met the requirements of India from a democratic and progressive standpoint.

What is a sustainable policy option today in terms of winning peace and stability in the subcontinent? The key lies in stopping, and rolling back, a process of nuclear weaponization that is yet fully to be under way. India's top priority must be to commit itself to the non-induction and non-deployment of nuclear weapons. Pakistan, facing enormous constraints in continuing with any serious programme of nuclear weaponization, has stated more than once that it sees no need to deploy nuclear weapons provided that India agrees not to do so. Other major steps that need urgently to be taken to resolve the perilous situation brought on by Pokhran-II and the India–Pakistan nuclear standoff are discussed in the concluding section of this tract.

These steps will also ensure that missiles and strike aircraft that are currently in use will not be suspect as nuclear weapon delivery systems. Further confidence-building measures will also be necessary to ensure that conventional missile capability in particular does not act as a destabilizing factor in the future.

The moratorium on testing that is in place needs to be continued and strengthened, preferably through the adoption of a resolution or an Act of Parliament. This will effectively curb the tendency on the part of hawkish forces as well as the scientific establishment in the atomic energy and defence research sectors to push nuclear weaponization outside the purview of democratic public scrutiny. Any attempt to tamper with the fundamentals of nuclear policy will be subject to effective parliamentary supervision. Such a policy will provide little room for intervention by U.S. imperialism and its allies in security issues in the subcontinent and also enable India to return to pursuing a serious agenda for global nuclear disarmament.

Unless India and Pakistan are agreed that nuclear non-deployment is a matter of top priority, there is no prospect of peace and stability in the subcontinent. This is the least that is owed to the 'one-sixth of humanity' in whose name the government of the Hindu Right cynically conducted its nuclear misadventure.

INDO–PAKISTAN DIALOGUE

The eleven claimed nuclear explosions in South Asia and the talk of weaponization, deterrents, second-strike capability, and deployment and use of nuclear weapons for 'self-defence' have introduced a dangerous new calculus in an already troubled India–Pakistan relationship. After the early euphoria vanished, after the initial flurry of intemperate language died down, and after infructuous official-level meetings ended in mutual recrimination, the realization grew at the government level in both countries that a process of top-level political dialogue must be initiated. Pressure for Indo–Pakistan talks covering a range of outstanding issues, including the nuclear mess and Kashmir, also came from the United States, the key 'interlocutor' who has been allowed to become an intervenor in South Asian nuclear affairs and, indirectly, in the India–Pakistan political relationship. With all this, the process of dialogue between India and Pakistan has picked up since October 1998. While this represents a positive political development, there is no room for complacency since little progress of substance has been made on the nuclear issue.

Even in the first round of talks between the Foreign Secretaries of the two countries, the mismatch or incompatibility between the official Indian and Pakistani positions on the question of reducing the nuclear threat became quite obvious. The central element of the

Indian side's approach was a mutual 'no-first-use' agreement, even before such a posture was officially announced at home. The Pakistan government's counter-proposal revolved round a general 'no war' pact together with negotiated reductions in both nuclear and conventional arms. Another key problem for India was Pakistan's attempt to link Kashmir to the nuclear issue. As we have seen, the problem was partly of the BJP-led government's making.

The level of India–Pakistan diplomacy was raised dramatically when a scheduled round of official-level talks was pre-empted by the inauguration of the Delhi–Lahore bus service by Prime Minister Vajpayee on February 20, 1999 and his subsequent meeting with his Pakistani counterpart, Nawaz Sharif, at Lahore. Given the proximity in time between the announcement of the plan for a bus ride to the border and a Prime Ministerial meeting in Lahore and the just concluded visit of the U.S. Deputy Secretary of State, Strobe Talbott, to both capitals, one may reasonably suspect a nexus between the two. In any case, the United States, in its role as *de facto* mediator on the nuclear issue in the subcontinent, had been insistent on progress being made by India and Pakistan bilaterally to reduce the nuclear danger in the subcontinent.

The Vajpayee–Sharif meeting generated substantial interest and enthusiasm in both India and Pakistan, revealing afresh that a meaningful agenda for peace and stability can count on a large popular constituency in both countries (notwithstanding some attempts by chauvinistic Right-wing political elements in Pakistan to make trouble during the Vajpayee visit). But on the nuclear issue, the Lahore exercise was long on rhetoric and short on substance.

The Lahore dialogue produced three documents: the 20-paragraph Lahore Declaration, an eight-point Joint Statement and an eight-point Memorandum of Understanding (MoU).[8]

The Declaration refers to the nuclear issue in the following terms. The Prime Ministers, recognizing 'that the nuclear dimension of the security environment of the two countries adds to their responsibility for avoidance of conflict between the two countries', agreed that their governments 'shall take immediate steps for reducing the risk or unauthorized use of nuclear weapons and discuss concepts and doctrines with a view to elaborating measures for confidence building in the nuclear and conventional fields, aimed at prevention of conflict'.

The Joint Statement basically communicates the top-level decision to systematize the dialogue, notably through periodic meetings of the Foreign Ministers of the two countries 'to discuss issues of mutual concern, including nuclear-related issues'.

So far as the nuclear issue is concerned, the MoU signed by the two Foreign Secretaries seems to be the document of most substance. This records the agreement of the two sides to

'engage in bilateral consultations on security concepts, and nuclear doctrines, with a view to developing measures for confidence building in the nuclear and conventional fields, aimed at avoidance of conflict';

'undertake to provide each other with advance notification in respect of ballistic missile flight tests' and to 'conclude a bilateral agreement in this regard';

undertake 'national measures to reduce the risks of accidental or unauthorized use of nuclear weapons under their respective control'; 'notify each other immediately in the event of any accidental, unauthorized or unexplained incident that could create the risk of a fall-out with adverse consequences for both sides, or an outbreak of a nuclear war between the two countries'; 'adopt measures aimed at diminishing the possibility of such actions or such incidents being misinterpreted by the other'; and 'identify/establish the appropriate communication mechanism for this purpose';

'continue to abide by their respective unilateral moratorium on conducting further nuclear test explosions unless either side, in exercise of its national sovereignty, decides that extraordinary events have jeopardized its supreme interests';

conclude an agreement on 'prevention of incidents at sea in order to ensure safety of navigation by naval vessels and aircraft belonging to the two sides';

'periodically . . . review the implementation of existing Confidence Building Measures (CBMs) and where necessary, set up appropriate consultative mechanisms to monitor and ensure effective implementation of these CBMs';

undertake a 'review of the existing communication links (e.g. between the respective Directors-General, Military Operations) with a view to upgrading and improving these links, and to provide for fail-safe and secure communications'; and

'engage in bilateral consultations on security, disarmament and non-proliferation issues within the context of negotiations on these issues in multilateral fora'.

The Lahore Declaration and the MoU reiterate the recognition by both sides that 'an environment of peace and security is in the supreme national interest of both sides' and that 'the resolution of all outstanding issues, including Jammu and Kashmir, is essential for this purpose'. The Joint Statement records progress made on the matter of liberalizing the visa and travel regime between the two countries and raises the hope of some modest bilateral cooperation and consultation in a few other fields.

On the nuclear issue, however, the key message of the Declaration and the MoU is that the two governments are bent on holding the course towards nuclear weaponization, whatever be the political, social and economic costs. As far as the Indian official position is concerned, an agenda calling for a national commitment not to induct and deploy nuclear weapons is simply not up for discussion.

Thus, on any fair reading, the leading share of responsibility for the failure of the Lahore exercise to achieve real progress towards resolving the India–Pakistan nuclear standoff rests with the BJP-led government. The fact is that in the months preceding the Lahore meeting of the Prime Ministers, the Pakistan government indicated its willingness, in effect, to discuss with the Indian side the non-deployment of nuclear weapons by India and Pakistan in tandem. Pakistan's Foreign Minister, Sartaj Aziz, offered in November 1998 that Pakistan would not deploy nuclear weapons if India took the same position, adding that deployment of such weapons was a 'reciprocal matter' between Islamabad and New Delhi.[9] This offer was reiterated on December 12, 1998 by Foreign Secretary Shamsher Ahmed in the context of a visit to Islamabad by U.S. Assistant Secretary of State, Karl Inderfurth.[10] Ahmed stated that if India did not deploy nuclear weapons or weaponize its nuclear capabilities, then Pakistan would not have any justification to do so. Some strategic affairs analysts and political commentators in the Indian media have speculated on Pakistan's motives for making the offer on non-deployment, but the fact remains that the Aziz offer is in principle the most far-going of the official proposals made thus far to find a way out of the India–Pakistan nuclear standoff . As for Prime Minister Vajpayee, for all his flowery rhetoric on peace and friendship, a matching response is not on the agenda.

The nuclear 'risk reduction' measures agreed on in principle at

Lahore are welcome in themselves. But they fall far short of the minimum requirement. They can even be characterized as moves designed to provide an illusory gloss of progress towards limiting the dangers of nuclear confrontation in the subcontinent. Essentially, the Declaration and the MoU promise that the two parties will play the deterrence game well and 'safely'. In practice, despite these promises, continuing with weaponization, as we have argued in detail, amounts to exposing the people of both countries to nuclear brinkmanship in the future. The assurances from Lahore are in large part a promise directed at the United States, other nuclear weapons states and economically powerful countries that have put strong diplomatic and economic pressure on India and Pakistan.

In the current scenario, it can be predicted that the bilateral consultations on security concepts and nuclear doctrines promised by both the Declaration and the MoU will be of little assistance in promoting peace and stability in South Asia. The nuclear defence postures of India and Pakistan are no secret. The nuclear policies of the government of the Hindu Right and of the Pakistan Muslim League government remain completely incompatible or mismatched. The mainstream of pro-weaponization Indian policy-makers emphasize nuclear weapons primarily as a strategic and political tool, as the currency of an illusory superpower status. The Pakistan state's rationale for weapons appears to have a more military, fighting-oriented flavour. Finding any common ground in these nuclear defence postures will be an extraordinary challenge.

The stage is undoubtedly being set for a continuing arms spiral in the subcontinent with a new, distinctly nuclear, edge to it. The Lahore Declaration and the MoU dispensed with even the standard disclaimer, common to recent policy pronouncements on South Asian nuclear issues, to the effect that India and Pakistan do not desire an arms race in the subcontinent. The sole positive step was the affirmation of each side's 'unilateral moratorium' on explosive testing, subject of course to the escape provision relating to extraordinary events jeopardizing national security. But given that the one thing the two governments agreed on was an eventual signing of the CTBT, the inclusion of this step was hardly surprising.

Propaganda hype has it that Vajpayee's bus diplomacy and the Lahore process brought about a sea-change in India–Pakistan relations in general and a breakthrough in the nuclear standoff specifically. But aside from the issues about nuclear weaponization we have discussed, two general points are worth remembering.

From the long history of imperialist behaviour during the Cold War, it is clear that the swings between periods of bellicose behaviour and aggressive rhetoric and periods of declarations of peace and the desire for friendship are part of the nuclear game. The swings were caused by a variety of factors, including domestic political compulsions, the need to reassure allies who had their specific concerns, and the pressure of popular struggles and movements against the massing of nuclear weapons and nuclear brinkmanship. Although on occasion, positive results were scored during periods of 'thaw' in the Cold War, nuclear arsenals remained awesomely real threats. If the political processes in India and Pakistan and their interaction on nuclear issues fail to produce a breakthrough in the nuclear standoff along the lines demanded in the last chapter below, the subcontinent will only witness a minor league replay of the Cold War game.

Secondly, the Sangh Parivar has played its own game in India of alternating aggressive behaviour with periods of seemingly more moderate conduct. Whether it be the building of the Ram temple at Ayodhya on the grave of the demolished Babri Masjid or the issue of 'conversions', the Parivar has used this strategy persistently. Those who read into Vajpayee's pacifist rhetoric at Lahore the message that the bellicosity of the Hindu Right on relations with Pakistan is behind us are living in a world of *maya*.

Hope for the future lies partly in the fact that, for all the extravagant claims made by the nuclear energy establishments and chauvinistic politicians, nuclear weaponization in both countries is likely to proceed slowly. There is time for new political leaderships in both countries to display the wisdom and the political courage necessary to draw the subcontinent back from the brink of grave nuclear folly.

CTBT *Comprehensive Test Ban Treaty*

7

WHY NOT JOIN THE CTBT AND THE FMCT?

It is an open secret that the eight rounds of talks between Jaswant Singh, the Indian Prime Minister's special representative and subsequently External Affairs Minister, and Strobe Talbott, U.S. Deputy Secretary of State, have been essentially about crafting and dressing up the terms of capitulation to the Discriminatory Global Nuclear Bargain so that economic sanctions, political pressures, and general arm-twisting can be withdrawn. The crux of the deal will be acceding to the CTBT and the far more demanding Fissile Material Cutoff Treaty (FMCT)-to-come while maintaining the pretence, for home consumption, that the government's claimed nuclear weapons status has gained some kind of unstated acceptance by the United States and the DGNB.

Left to itself, the Vajpayee government would have signed the CTBT in 1998 as the first big step towards meeting the terms of capitulation. This would have been followed by working closely with the United States and its allies in the Conference on Disarmament in Geneva to expedite the conclusion of the FMCT on terms envisaged by the DGNB.

But acceding to the CTBT involved a major political risk for the BJP. Its political opponents, the Left parties, the Congress(I), per-

DGNB *Discriminatory Global Nuclear Bargain*

haps some other opposition parties, influential sections of the media, and various circles involved in the nuclear policy debate of 1995–96 would call a sell-out when they saw one. In addition, a section of nuclear hawks, especially those in the RSS who wanted India to proceed defiantly along the path of weaponization by conducting more tests and refusing to accept any restraints on fissile material production, would be displeased, even if one assumed that they could eventually be brought round to accepting the government's decision.[1]

THE CTBT DEBATE

A wide-ranging political debate on the CTBT had taken place in 1995–96, an unusual example of a many-sided, comprehensive public debate on an issue of major importance. The BJP, along with the Janata Dal, the Congress(I) and the Left parties, had then taken a strong stand against the CTBT, making for a rare national consensus in policy-making. The objections to the treaty were discussed in depth and sold so aggressively to the country, that two unilateralists, Praful Bidwai and Achin Vanaik, have alleged that the outcome of the debate was a 'terrible distortion of the very terms of discourse on the CTBT issue'. Indeed Bidwai and Vanaik denounce the 1995–96 public debate as 'one of the most shameful, deceitful, ignorant . . . on any issue in the last 50 years in India'.[2]

The CTBT was, as strategic affairs analyst C. Raja Mohan put, 'designed to preserve the hegemony of the nuclear weapons powers', 'put a cap on India's nuclear capability', override 'India's disarmament and security concerns', and subject it to the 'worst form of political blackmail'.[3] Or, as he summed up elsewhere:

> India must be reconciled to three central facts. Even with a little more disarmament embroidery, the CTBT will not take the world even one step closer towards nuclear abolition. Second, the treaty is, in essence, a non-proliferation arrangement and one of its principal effects is to place a qualitative cap on the nuclear potential of India. Third, even if India agrees to join the CTBT, the effort of the West to denuclearize India will not stop. It will move from the CTBT to a fissile material cut-off treaty that imposes a quantitative cap on India's nuclear programme. If India succumbs to that, the next step is to roll back and eliminate India's nuclear and missile capabilities. It will be wise for India to draw the line now rather than get on to the slippery slope of denuclearization.[4]

DGNB *Discriminatory Global Nuclear Bargain*

Nor were punches pulled at the official level. At a press conference in New York on August 30, 1996, Ambassador Prakash Shah, India's Permanent Representative to the United Nations, characterized the treaty as 'a flawed document that not only does not meet India's concerns, but even fails to meet the terms of the mandate given to the CTBT'. He explained that the treaty failed to win a consensus at the Conference on Disarmament in Geneva, did not place the banning of nuclear tests within a nuclear disarmament framework, and remained 'merely an extension of the exercise to limit horizontal nuclear proliferation'. It failed to 'stop development of nuclear weapons or their qualitative improvement by the nuclear weapons countries'.

Ambassador Shah also set out India's vision of a genuine test ban treaty in elegant terms:

> (a) such a treaty should be securely anchored in a global disarmament contract and linked through treaty language to the elimination of weapons in a time-bound framework; (b) it should end all nuclear weapons development be it explosive-based or non-explosive-based; and (c) it should not provide a licence, such as was provided by the indefinitely extended Nuclear Non-Proliferation Treaty, to proliferate nuclear weapons. [5]

In the delusional haze that was a byproduct of the Pokhran explosions, the first official statements of the Vajpayee government gave the impression that, with the magic weapons in hand, it was going to try to rewrite the CTBT, if not the NPT regime itself. This posture then faded to fuzzy rhetoric to the effect that there was no question of signing the CTBT without conditions or in its present form. On May 14, 1998, Vajpayee solemnly assured opposition leaders that his Government would not sign the CTBT 'unconditionally'.[6] This naturally made informed persons wonder what sort of conditions or concessions might be wrested from a multilateral treaty that had been signed by 150 countries, or what alternative form of the treaty would be open for India to sign in the conceivable future.

But the subsequent explication by Prime Minister Vajpayee, his advisers, and some strategic affairs apologists (who, reversing or obscuring their old arguments, decided that India must join the CTBT and also the FMCT-to-come) made it clear that the 'conditions', or rather concessions, supposedly being negotiated had nothing to do with the CTBT. They were, in fact, irrelevant to the CTBT issue. It

NPT *Nuclear Non-Proliferation Treaty* FMCT *Fissile Material Cut-Off Treaty*

was suggested that India would somehow win, after it signed the CTBT, an end to the international technological blockade, access to dual use and even nuclear technology, eventual acceptance of India's new nuclear position, and so forth.

In reality, the suggestion that accession to the CTBT involved some major *quid pro quo* was a hoax that was being played on the Indian people.

THE HOAX IN PROGRESS

To understand the nature of the hoax, let us first look at the political demands the United States, backed by various other powerful countries, has publicly pressed on India in the aftermath of the Pokhran nuclear explosions. The three key demands are: (1) sign and ratify the CTBT quickly and without conditions; (2) participate positively and on the basis of the agreed mandate in the negotiations at the Conference on Disarmament on the FMCT; and (3) undo the nuclear weaponization and the missile programme announced, and do not deploy nuclear weapons or missiles capable of delivering them. Post-Chagai, the same demands were pressed on Pakistan; India, however, was identified as the principal target.

The full western agenda was unveiled when the Foreign Ministers of the P-5, the United States, the United Kingdom, France, the Russian Federation, and China, met on June 4, 1998. The Geneva meeting formulated a bill of particulars that would, within days, be adopted by the United Nations Security Council in an unprecedented resolution. Six days later came a further escalation of the demands made on India and Pakistan. The June 12 communiqué of the G-8 Foreign Ministers, meeting in London, used language blunter and more peremptory than anything used against India in an international forum over the past twenty-five years.[7]

After condemning the nuclear tests carried out by India and Pakistan, the G-8 Foreign Ministers demanded that the two countries 'should immediately take' the following steps endorsed by the UN Security Council:

'stop all further nuclear tests' and adhere to the CTBT 'immediately and unconditionally', thereby facilitating its early entry into force;

'refrain from weaponization or deployment of nuclear weapons and from the testing or deployment of missiles capable of delivering nuclear weapons, and enter into firm commitments not to weaponize or deploy nuclear

CTBT *Comprehensive Test Ban Treaty* FMCT *Fissile Material Cut-Off Treaty*

weapons or missiles';

'refrain from any further production of fissile material for nuclear weapons or other nuclear explosive devices and participate, in a positive spirit and on the basis of the agreed mandate', in negotiations with other states at the Conference on Disarmament on the FMCT 'with a view to reaching early agreement'; and

'confirm their policies not to export equipment, materials and technology that would contribute to weapons of mass destruction or missiles capable of delivering them, and undertake appropriate commitments in this regard'.

In the process, the G-8 Foreign Ministers, building on the stand taken at the Geneva meeting of the P-5 and in the UN Security Council, underlined their commitment to the NPT as 'the cornerstone of the non-proliferation regime'. They also rubbed in the point that 'notwithstanding those tests, India and Pakistan do not have the status of nuclear weapons states in accordance with the NPT'.

It strained credulity for anyone to suggest that the United States or the P-5 or the G-8 or those who subscribed to the UN Security Council resolution were ready to give up the core political position set out in these tough public documents.

The U.S. response to the policy confusion in New Delhi, and to the natural swing in the policy towards capitulation to the DGNB, has been to play upon the Indian government's allergy to sanctions to pursue its objective. Economic sanctions were first marginally relaxed in a few areas, but in a manner that appeared deliberately to tilt against India in favour of Pakistan.[8] The slight relaxation of the sanctions approach was followed by the clamping down of a demoralizing 'entities list', which barred U.S. companies from trading with some 40 Indian entities and 200 subsidiaries.[9] Subsequently, an on-again, off-again approach by the executive branch, interacting with lobbies and caucuses in the Congress, has created a good deal of confusion in India, especially within pro-weaponization circles and in the media. It has also induced a remarkable obsession with the nuances of thinking on economic sanctions by individual Congressmen.

To make matters worse, during the run-up to the seventh round of the dialogue with Jaswant Singh, Deputy Secretary of State Talbott publicly spelt out what the U.S. expected from the dialogue, embarrassing the Vajpayee government greatly and giving the lie to the sug-

DGNB *Discriminatory Global Nuclear Bargain*

gestion that there would be some kind of pragmatic Western acceptance of India's '*de facto*' nuclear weapon status. In a well-timed November 1998 address delivered at the Brookings Institution in Washington D.C., Talbott declared that 'we do not and will not concede, even by implication, that India and Pakistan have established themselves as nuclear weapons states under the NPT'.[10] In this address and also in a lengthy article published in *The Times of India*, the State Department official let the cat out of the bag by specifying the 'five practical steps' the United States was 'working intently' with India and Pakistan to 'encourage' them to take:

Sign and ratify the CTBT quickly.

Halt all production of fissile material that can be used for nuclear weapons, in anticipation of the early conclusion of an FMCT in Geneva.

Accept 'prudent, mutually reinforcing restraints' on the development, flight testing, and storage of missiles capable of carrying nuclear weapons, and also on the basing of nuclear-capable aircraft.

Bring export control policies and regimes relating to sensitive material and technologies that could be used in the development of weapons of mass destruction 'up to international standards'.

Address the 'underlying causes' of Indo–Pakistan tension and nuclear competition by 'direct, high-level, frequent and above all, productive dialogue' to 'liberate' India and Pakistan from their mutual 'enmity'.

Talbott also held out the 'near certainty' of a decline in the flow of foreign capital to India and Pakistan, as 'risk-averse' investors backed away from 'what will look like an unpredictable environment', as 'perhaps the most serious economic threat'.[11]

The United States played upon the sanctions-related anxieties, expectations and nervousness of the Vajpayee government as though on a piano. Talbott's blunt explication of U.S. political demands appears to have caused considerable unhappiness and discomfiture to the BJP-led government. This was clear from Vajpayee's 1998 Assembly election campaign criticism of, even attacks on, American policy and its double standards on the question of nuclear weapons. Subsequently, following the eighth round of Indo–U.S. talks on India's nuclear adventure, Secretary of State Madeleine Albright made a public assertion that 'India and Pakistan have expressed their willingness to sign the Comprehensive Test Ban Treaty'.[12] The Vajpayee government, which had denied repeatedly that it had given any such

NPT *Nuclear Non-Proliferation Treaty* CTBT *Comprehensive Test Ban Treaty* assurance to the United States, found that the cat had once again been let out of the bag.

INDIA'S OBJECTIONS TO THE CTBT

Let us now review the precise reasons for India refusing to sign the CTBT in 1996, and consider with an open mind whether these reasons either disappeared or weakened sufficiently for the CTBT to be signed after Pokhran-II. The core objection, as spelt out in Geneva and New York by the Government of India's articulate representatives, was that the CTBT – as a corollary of the discriminatory NPT regime – failed to meet the test of both India's disarmament objectives and its security concerns.

Article I of the treaty prohibits state parties from conducting 'any nuclear weapon test explosions or any other nuclear explosion'. On the basis of the negotiating record, this is understood to include all nuclear explosions with yields above zero, in accordance with U.S. President Bill Clinton's August 1995 proposal. Article IV and the verification protocol provide for a tough verification regime. This will rest on an International Monitoring System and on-site inspections that could, under certain circumstances (as Iraq's experience has shown), prove unacceptably intrusive. Then there is the near-coercive Article XIV which provides for Entry Into Force (EIF). What Article XIV means for India is that its ratification of the CTBT (along with ratification by 43 other states specified for possessing nuclear power and research reactors) has been made a specific condition for EIF. The effective deadline was fixed as September 24, 1999, that is, three years after the CTBT was opened for signature.

1. *Discrimination*. Against such a draft treaty, the first and predictable Indian objection was that the nuclear weapons states led by the United States were bent on perpetuating the discriminatory nuclear order DGNB. It was, in the words of Ambassador Shah, 'an extension of the exercise to limit horizontal nuclear proliferation'. 'Designed', as Raja Mohan put it, 'to preserve the hegemony of the nuclear weapon powers', the CTBT was unacceptable to India, which was resolutely opposed to discrimination in nuclear affairs. One of its 'principal effects' as a non-proliferation arrangement would be 'to place a qualitative cap on the nuclear potential of India'.[13]

DGNB *Discriminatory Global Nuclear Bargain*

Quite obviously, this basic feature of the CTBT remains; it was only the BJP-led government's stand, and the stand of strategic affairs analysts, that took a 180-degree turn. Now we are being instructed, by both old and new apologists for the CTBT, that the treaty is not at all discriminatory because, unlike the NPT, it places the same obligations on all member signatories. As if we, and diplomats like Arundhati Ghose, who in 1996 characterized it as a corollary of the discriminatory NPT, did not know that! As if the real Indian objection was not that the effects of the CTBT obligations placed on nuclear weapons states and the rest would be profoundly different.

2. *No time-bound disarmament commitment*. The second official Indian objection was that the nuclear weapons states, led by the United States, were refusing to commit themselves to any time-bound disarmament schedule. Instead, they had provided themselves, in the words of Ambassador Shah, with 'a licence . . . to proliferate nuclear weapons' through 'the indefinitely extended Nuclear Non-Proliferation Treaty'.

Obviously, this fundamental flaw in the CTBT – the absence of any linkage with a time-bound global disarmament contract – remains, except that official policy now seeks to extend the 'licence' to India.

3. *Built-in loopholes*. The third Indian objection to the CTBT was that the nuclear weapons states, especially the United States, had written into the treaty loopholes that would permit them to continue refining and developing their nuclear arsenals at their test sites and in their laboratories, while maintaining their active stockpiles. The CTBT prohibited all nuclear explosions above zero yield. However, sophisticated SCEs, computer simulation and the development of frontier technologies, which are not banned, would enable the advanced nuclear weapons states to refine and upgrade their nuclear arsenals.

Countering the 'fantastic claims' made in India confusing the CTBT with 'a disarmament measure', Raja Mohan asserted that for the U.S. establishment 'it helps freeze the hierarchy among the nuclear weapon powers in favour of the U.S. . . . [and] helps limit the strategic capabilities of the only possible challenger to future American dominance, China. . . . [It] will be the first step in capping and even-

CTBT *Comprehensive Test Ban Treaty* NPT *Nuclear Non-Proliferation Treaty* SCE *Sub-Critical Experiment*

tually rolling back the nuclear potentials of emerging powers like India'. He pointed out that under a no-test regime, 'the American lead in computer simulation helps it keep way ahead of its allies and likely adversaries among the nuclear five' and also helped the three western nuclear weapons states, the U.S., the U.K. and France, to 'deepen their cooperation in computer simulation of nuclear weapons under the leadership of America'.[14]

Clearly, this differential, and discriminatory, effect of the CTBT ban on above zero yield nuclear explosions could not have changed in favour of India as a result of the five Pokhran explosions, the data they have yielded, and the scientific capabilities they have established. In Chapter 5 we showed that the official claims about current and emerging Indian nuclear weapons capabilities are seriously exaggerated. Notwithstanding the claims to 'shakti', Pokhran-II has done little to overcome the asymmetry between Indian nuclear capabilities and the capabilities of the five nuclear weapons states. The United States retains an undiminished, perhaps widening, scientific and technological lead with respect to nuclear weapons under a CTBT regime.

4. *Coercive EIF clause*. India strenuously objected to the near-coercive Article XIV, which provides that if the CTBT has not entered into force by September 24, 1999, the states that have ratified the treaty shall meet in a Conference that will consider the situation and 'decide by consensus what measures consistent with international law may be undertaken to accelerate the ratification process in order to facilitate the early entry into force of this Treaty'. Even the NPT does not have this draconian provision for EIF. In effect, by throwing the entire burden of the CTBT coming into force on India's shoulders, by making India accountable for the treaty not entering into force and for the consequences of that occurrence, and by fixing a deadline, Article XIV of the CTBT represents a direct attempt to erode India's sovereignty and also an ultimatum.

5. *National security concerns*. The final Indian objection to the CTBT concerned India's national security. In his statement of August 22, 1996 made in Geneva, External Affairs Minister I.K. Gujral mentioned, among other objections, 'certain national security concerns' which 'make it impossible for us to subscribe to a draft CTBT

EIF *entry into force*

that is merely an instrument for horizontal non-proliferation rather than disarmament'.[15] India's security concerns 'oblige us to maintain our nuclear option'. While pointing out that the country had exercised 'unparalleled restraint' in not carrying out nuclear explosions after 1974 and in refraining from 'weaponizing our option', Gujral declared that 'we cannot accept constraints on our option as long as nuclear weapons states continue to rely on their nuclear arsenals for their security'.

A week later, Ambassador Shah, pointing out that India was the only country that had observed a voluntary moratorium on nuclear tests since 1974, asserted in New York: 'Our opposition to this document has nothing to do with any change in our policy in continuing this moratorium'. Ambassador Arundhati Ghose followed this up with the assertion that 'India's security would best be guaranteed by the elimination of nuclear weapons'.[16]

Vajpayee's parliamentary statement of May 27, 1998, as well as the supporting policy paper, asserted that the 'primary reason' for refusing to sign the CTBT was the assessment that India's national security concerns remained unaddressed.[17] This amounted to rewriting the recent historical record and airbrushing out of the policy other vital elements of what was, after all, a widely known position.

WHAT THE FMCT WILL REQUIRE

Pokhran-II placed India's nuclear policy on the slippery slope to joining the FMCT, which is being negotiated in Geneva. One has only to read the research articles available on the web-site of the Institute of Defence Studies and Analyses (IDSA), New Delhi to understand how strongly, and why, the Indian government and the nuclear policy establishment opposed such a treaty in the past.[18] It is clear that the FMCT, which will prohibit all further production of fissile material – highly enriched uranium (HEU) and plutonium – for weapons purposes, or outside safeguards, in all countries is designed *inter alia* to restrain and cap India's nuclear programme and stop the country's progress on the learning curve.[19]

The pre-Pokhran-II official policy understanding was that such a treaty would be even worse for the Indian nuclear programme than the CTBT. In the first place, like the CTBT, it would be designed as

CTBT *Comprehensive Test Ban Treaty* FMCT *Fissile Material Cut-Off Treaty*

a discriminatory non-proliferation control arrangement, not at all as an arms control or disarmament initiative. The object would especially be to cap the nuclear stocks and capabilities of threshold states like India. On top of their nuclear arsenals, the five nuclear weapons states are sitting on huge stocks of weapons grade fissile material. In their own determination (with the possible exception of China), there is no need for any further production of fissile material for weapons purposes; indeed, the abundance of existing fissile material stocks is a subject of serious environmental concern in these countries. In fact, all five nuclear weapons states have declared that they have stopped producing highly enriched uranium and plutonium for weapons purposes.

Secondly, the FMCT would provide for a far tougher, more intrusive verification or safeguards regime than the CTBT. If it joins the FMCT, India will have to place its nuclear programme prospectively under full-scope safeguards, that is, external controls on all its nuclear installations and activities. With only existing fissile material stock exempted from the external control regime, this arrangement will undermine, and make nonsense of, India's decision to stay outside the NPT regime, unless the cynical assumption is made that the only reason for keeping out of the NPT was to put away unsafeguarded fissile material for a small arsenal of nuclear weapons.

Although the FMCT negotiations at the Conference on Disarmament had been delayed on account of certain technical differences among the nuclear weapons states and some policy-based resistance from developing countries, it is clear that the Pokhran-II and Chagai explosions kickstarted the stalled negotiations and made them a matter of higher priority for the United States and its allies.

The changed stance on the FMCT constitutes further evidence that nuclear policy under the regime of the Hindu Right swung very quickly from adventurism to virtual surrender to the DGNB.

The essence of the strategy of the government of the Hindu Right has been to try and hang on to *de facto* nuclear weaponization at any cost. Primarily, this involves , in the words of Praful Bidwai, a consistent voice against nuclear weaponization, 'a shady nuclear bargain with the United States which would allow New Delhi to keep its nuclear weapons in return for abandoning the global nuclear disar-

NPT *Nuclear Non-Proliferation Treaty* DGNB *Discriminatory Global Nuclear Bargain*

mament agenda'.[20] From a democratic standpoint, the pursuit of nuclear weaponization while surrendering to the CTBT and the FMCT-to-come, and being co-opted into the discriminatory global nuclear order as a minor partner, must be recognized as the worst possible turn India's nuclear policy could have taken.

CTBT *Comprehensive Test Ban Treaty* FMCT *Fissile Material Cut-Off Treaty*

8

GETTING OFF THE TIGER: AN AGENDA FOR DEWEAPONIZATION

Let us now put together the conclusions from the factual material, arguments, and analysis presented above. In Chapter 1, we saw Pokhran-II and its follow-up in a political context; identified the destabilizing, tension-raising and other negative effects; examined the motivation behind the nuclear adventure; and called attention to the quick, natural swing of the nuclear policy of the government of the Hindu Right from adventurism towards capitulation to the terms laid down by the enforcers of the discriminatory global nuclear order. In Chapter 2, we attempted to answer the reasonable question, 'When others have it, why shouldn't India?' This we did by first reviewing the character and size of the world's nuclear weapons arsenals and the absolute refusal by nuclear weapons states, above all by U.S. imperialism, to make any commitment to eliminate nuclear weapons over a time frame; and then looking, from a scientific angle, at the nature of nuclear weapons and the monstrous horror, and unwinnability, of nuclear war. What was achieved through Pokhran-II and its follow-up was the exposure of the people of India and Pakistan to the infinite horrors that nuclear weapons can inflict. In a brief aside, we presented a ballpark estimate of the economic costs of Indian nuclear weaponization (Rs 40,000 crores to Rs 50,000 crores, over a ten-year period) from preliminary work done by a few economists. We concluded that the total economic burden, involving direct as well as indirect costs, would be huge. Although not the primary argument against nuclear weaponization, and our discussion has been correspondingly brief, the economic burden is an important objection that raises issues of vital importance for the Indian people. In Chapter 3, we highlighted the fallacies and contradictions of the theory of deterrence – which depends on the possessor's willingness actually to use nuclear weapons – citing expert evidence to show that the theory is both false and dangerous. We argued that Vajpayee's embrace of the doctrine of deterrence at the end of the twentieth century was a textbook case of *akratic* adherence to a chauvinist ideology driving away common sense, and that the Indian *avatar* of the doctrine, 'minimum credible nuclear deterrent', made a mockery of half a century of sound policy-making. We pointed out that the chorus of support for the doctrine of deterrence from the pro-weaponization lobby, chiefly the strategic affairs community, the leadership of the atomic energy and defence research establishments, and a few retired high-ranking military officers, marks a low point in the history of India's nuclear policy.

Addressing in detail, in Chapter 4, the question of whether Pokhran-II and attempted nuclear weaponization represent continuity with longstanding Indian nuclear policy, we concluded that they are a reactionary departure from a well-conceived and tested policy that served India's interests well for half a century – through a balanced commitment to independence and peace. Interrogating India's nuclear policy, past and present, also helped to answer the question, 'When others have it, why shouldn't India?' In Chapter 5, we refuted the claim that Pokhran-II was, in scientific terms, a great and glorious achievement. We reviewed and deplored the pro-active, often hawkish and weapons-friendly political role that certain senior scientists of the nuclear establishment have played over a period of many years. Examining India's nuclear weapons capabilities *vis-à-vis* the claims made by the nuclear energy and defence research establishments, we found gross exaggerations and misleading assertions that could lead policy-making further astray. We concluded our scientifically informed section on nuclear capabilities with the observation that India's (and, by extension, Pakistan's) current nuclear status is best characterized as 'pseudo-weaponized'. It follows that it is not too late to reverse this dangerous and dishonourable course.

In Chapter 6, we examined Pokhran-II's core defence: the claim that it was necessitated by supreme national security interests. We demonstrated that, far from securing India and its people in any sense, the nuclear adventure has achieved the very opposite of what the government of the Hindu Right and all shades of nuclear hawks claimed. We noted the heightened danger to peace and stability arising from the adventurist testing of Agni II and Pakistan's immediate response. After critically examining the elaborations and refinements of official nuclear weapons policy after Pokhran-II and the specifics of the Lahore exercise, we concluded that, on the one hand, such a policy course is benighted and, on the other, the steps agreed upon in the three texts that came out of the summit meeting of the Prime Ministers of India and Pakistan fall far short of what is required to get off the nuclear tiger. In Chapter 7, we mapped the swing of the BJP-led government's nuclear policy from adventurism towards surrender to the discriminatory global nuclear order. In particular, we explored the implications of the 180-degree turn on the CTBT and the FMCT, both corollaries of the Nuclear Non-Proliferation Treaty. We demonstrated that in the process the United States, supposed to play the role of a key *interlocutor* (for both India and Pakistan), has actually emerged as an *intervenor* that is determined to shape the terms of India's nuclear policy and of the new Indo–Pakistan equation. In this chapter, we also looked at the CTBT in relation to scientific issues and at U.S. imperialism's plans to refine and upgrade its nuclear arsenal under a CTBT regime.

This detailed analysis is meant to show why a nuclear policy that has turned hawkish and landed itself in deep trouble presents a live and present danger to peace, security and stability in India and South Asia. It is simultaneously a threat to the basic interests, well-being and future of the Indian people. (A similar observation can be made about Pakistan's nuclear policy.) The dangerous policy cannot bail itself out, or be allowed to do so, by sacrificing well-established principles and swinging to the other extreme of foreclosing India's independence in the sphere of nuclear policy.

An objective assessment of what has happened since May 11, 1998 points to what needs to be done. The principal issue before the

CTBT *Comprehensive Test Ban Treaty* FMCT *Fissile Material Cut-Off Treaty*

people of India is not the CTBT, it is the political, moral, social, and economic unacceptability of nuclear weaponization – and its abhorrent accompaniment, the doctrine of nuclear deterrence, and in the Indian case, the tragi-comic doctrine of the 'minimum credible nuclear deterrent'. This must be fully understood by democratic campaigns. From the early days following Pokhran-II, when scenes of celebration on the streets of India were flashed on television screens across the world, political India has come a long way in figuring out and opposing the Hindu Right's adventure of riding the nuclear tiger. The BJP was not able to gain any electoral or political mileage from the adventure; on the contrary, the effects and implications of Pokhran-II made life much more difficult for the 13-month Vajpayee government. This offers a good lesson for any future government in India that might be tempted to gain political mileage from such adventures.

The nuclear weaponization attempted by the Hindu Right must be rolled back – through concerted peace-oriented and democratic political opposition, which also means determined public pressure and action. The authors and apologists of Pokhran-II claim that nuclear weaponization is a *fait accompli* and that nobody, in India or abroad, will be able to reverse this. This is patently untrue, as the detailed material, especially the scientific assessment and analysis, presented in this tract demonstrates. The Pokhran and Chagai nuclear explosions cannot be undone, but nuclear weaponization in India and Pakistan can be.

The broad-based democratic campaign against nuclear weaponization must not allow itself to become complacent: it must not make the mistake of assuming that since the Hindu Right has done badly out of Pokhran-II, the issue has been decisively won. Even after changes of regime in New Delhi, the challenge of rolling back nuclear weaponization that has, at least partially, been put in place will remain. So will the necessity to resist external pressures and U.S.-led attempts to put an end to the independence of India's nuclear policy.

Fortunately, giving up the path of nuclear weaponization and deployment will be a democratically verifiable process, especially in a country like India. Whether an Indian government goes along, or turns away from, such a path is unlikely to remain a secret for a pro-

CTBT *Comprehensive Test Ban Treaty*

longed period, given the multiple actors involved, including an active political opposition and press. Nevertheless, the democratic campaign must demand in the interest of the Indian people an end to the nuclear opacity and secrecy that the atomic energy and defence research establishments, backed by the political government, might insist on maintaining.

The campaign must also meet head on the authoritarian concept of national security embraced by the Hindu Right and by all shades of nuclear hawks. As against such a concept, which projects an understanding of India's security purely in the military sense of the term, a democratic and just concept of security for the people in an all-round sense must be promoted. The defence forces have their due place in such a scheme, but security for the people must essentially be understood as securing their livelihood, their food and other basic needs, their entitlement to the fruits of their labour and development, their political and human rights in the fullest sense, and a sustainable future.

The democratic campaign must look ahead clear-sightedly and work out the principal demands, in specifics and in order of priority, that are to be pressed on Indian nuclear policy now and for the intermediate future. It must also sequence the de-weaponizing steps demanded in a way that makes good sense.

This tract proposes that five principal demands be pressed on the Government of India for now and the intermediate future. In achievable sequence and order of priority, they are:

Non-deployment and non-induction of nuclear weapons. (Deployment is fitting nuclear warheads onto delivery systems, that is, certain types of aircraft, ballistic missiles or submarines. Induction is giving nuclear weapons to the armed forces and training them in nuclear warfare.)

Non-conversion of fissile material stocks, that is, plutonium or enriched uranium, into nuclear weapons.

No further nuclear explosive testing.

Abjuring the doctrine of nuclear deterrence, and the Indian variant of the 'minimum credible nuclear deterrent', and returning to the path of active advocacy of global nuclear disarmament, in close cooperation with other developing countries.

Dismantling and destroying the nuclear weapons in the small arsenal.

These major steps, but especially the first and the fifth, need to be taken in tandem or cooperation with Pakistan. For obvious reasons, a commitment not to deploy nuclear weapons must be grasped as the first priority. Pakistan's government has already indicated that it is willing to agree not to deploy nuclear weapons if the Indian government will make the same commitment. It was the BJP–RSS commitment to a Hindu Rashtra armed with deliverable nuclear weapons and also to a second-strike capability that stood in the way of agreeing to non-deployment. Obviously, non-induction or de-induction of nuclear weapons will make sense only if non-deployment is achieved. The moratorium on nuclear testing announced by the Indian government must be continued; it can be firmed up by a resolution, perhaps even an Act, of Parliament that has the support of all political parties.[1] Likewise, a commitment not to weaponize fissile material stocks that are in hand or will be produced in the future can be made a firm policy tenet; it can also be underwritten by a resolution or an Act of Parliament.

Dismantling or destroying the nuclear weapons in hand will be a tough demand to make on Indian nuclear policy. But it is the logical final step without which the democratic agenda of de-weaponization will be incomplete. It must not be confused with giving up the nuclear *option*, which Indian policy has consistently insisted on retaining from the time it came to reject the core of the Discriminatory Global Nuclear Bargain, the NPT. But accepting the demand to dismantle and destroy the nuclear weapons in what is, at most, a small arsenal will be an act of far-sightedness and courage for any government in India. It will be opposed and criticized by chauvinists and hawks, but will win tremendous goodwill and appreciation in democratic quarters everywhere. If South Africa could dismantle and destroy its six 'bombs in the basement' by mid-1993 in anticipation of the era of Nelson Mandela and with his firm support, so can India and Pakistan by the sane, sovereign and concerted choice of their peoples.[2]

Once the dangers and unacceptable costs of deployment and weaponization, and of a South Asian nuclear arms race, are decisively ended, other issues connected with India's international tasks and responsibilities in the field of nuclear disarmament can be examined afresh, and with an open mind. However, capitulating to the discriminatory global nuclear order through joining the CTBT and

NPT *Nuclear Non-Proliferation Treaty* CTBT *Comprehensive Test Ban Treaty* committing India to accession to an FMCT as envisaged by the United States and the P-5 while inducting and deploying nuclear weapons would be the worst possible option. So long as there is an insistence on building security on nuclear weapons and a 'minimum credible nuclear deterrent', there can be no way out of a volatile and dangerous situation.

It was clear from the start that the government of the Hindu Right would not be able to find a way to get off the nuclear tiger. A change of political regime in New Delhi appeared to be the *condition precedent* for this. The democratic campaign must press its five point agenda of de-weaponization vigorously, with an eye to the new opportunities offered by a change of government. Whatever a non-BJP successor government can or cannot do in other areas, whether it proves to be transitional or longer-lived, it will serve the people's interest decisively if it shows the political will and courage to undo nuclear weaponization in South Asia.

FMCT *Fissile Material Cut-Off Treaty*

NOTES

1 INTRODUCTION

[1] Comment by a top source within the nuclear energy establishment, quoted in 'The perils of nuclear adventurism', *Frontline*, June 5, 1998.

[2] Statement read out by Brajesh Mishra, Principal Secretary to the Prime Minister, at a New Delhi press conference on May 11, 1998; see *The Hindu*, May 12, 1998.

[3] Interview to Prabhu Chawla, *India Today* (May 25, 1998), released by the Prime Minister's Office (PMO) on May 15, 1998.

[4] This was the claim made by A.P.J. Abdul Kalam, Scientific Adviser to the Defence Minister and the key figure behind India's ballistic missile programme, at a press conference he, R. Chidambaram, Secretary of the Department of Atomic Energy and Chairman of the Atomic Energy Commission, and other top scientists addressed in New Delhi on May 17, 1998; see *The Hindu*, May 18, 1998.

[5] Union Home Minister L.K. Advani spelt out government policy thinking on the situation in Jammu and Kashmir on May 18. The new line was 'to deal firmly and strongly with Pakistan's hostile designs and activities in Kashmir' and even the option of 'hot pursuit' was not ruled out. Making the explicit assumption that India's 'decisive step to become a nuclear weapons state has brought about a qualitatively new stage in Indo–Pak[istan] relations, particularly in finding a lasting solution to the Kashmir problem', Advani called upon the Pakistan government to 'realize the change in the geo-strategic situation in the region and the world'. (*The Hindu*, May 19, 1998.) This was ten days before Pakistan conducted its Chagai nuclear explosions. It appears that during the interregnum some of the BJP leaders, or at least Advani, entertained the delusion that with Pokhran, India had acquired a strategic nuclear edge over Pakistan; they may have even believed that Islamabad was bluffing about its nuclear weapons capabilities.

[6] *Akrasia* in ancient Greek philosophy means not doing what you know to be right and, in fact, doing what you know to be wrong. There are varying explanations for *akratic* behaviour.

7 'Pak promises tit-for-tat, U.S. saddened', *The Hindustan Times*, April 12, 1999; 'Agni-II has derailed peace process: Sartaj Aziz', and ' Agni: a painful choice', *Dawn*, April 12, 1999.

8 Letter of May 11, 1998 from Prime Minister A.B. Vajpayee to U.S. President Bill Clinton, leaked immediately to *The New York Times* and published by it on May 13, 1998. The text of the letter was reproduced subsequently by several newspapers in India.

9 Aijaz Ahmad, 'The Hindutva weapon', *Frontline*, June 5, 1998.

10 N. Ram, 'India & China: What lies ahead?', *Frontline*, September 25, 1998.

11 For Fernandes' remarks see *The Times of India*, April 12, 1999. For the remarks by hawkish security analyst Brahma Chellaney, see Barry Bearak's report, 'India tests missiles able to hit deep into neighbour lands', *The New York Times*, April 12, 1999.

12 Prime Minister Nehru's view was: 'In essence today there is a conflict in the world between two things, the atom bomb and what it represents and the spirit of humanity'. Cited in A. K. Chopra, *India's Policy on Disarmament*, New Delhi: ABC Publishing House, 1984.

13 See Manpreet Sethi, 'The Struggle For Nuclear Disarmament', in *Nuclear India*, edited by Jasjit Singh, New Delhi: Knowledge World in association with the Institute For Defence Studies and Analyses, 1998, pp. 73–95.

14 Michael Foot, *Dr Strangeglove, I Presume*, London: Victor Gollancz, 1999, p. 109.

15 Mani Shankar Aiyar, 'Rajiv Gandhi and the CTBT: a reply', *The Hindu*, February 9, 1999.

16 See Jayati Ghosh, 'Sanctions and being sanctimonious', *Frontline*, June 19, 1998.

17 'U.S. looks to India's emergence as a global power', *The Times of India*, November 13, 1998.

18 See C. Rammanohar Reddy, 'The wages of Armageddon', three editorial page articles in *The Hindu*, August 31, September 1 and 2, 1998. See also his draft paper 'Cost of Nuclear Weaponization in India – Some Estimates'; and Jayati Ghosh, 'The Bomb, the Budget and the Economy', in *Out of Nuclear Darkness: The Indian Case For Disarmament*, New Delhi: MIND (Movement in India for Nuclear Disarmament), 1999, pp. 17–23.

19 Jayati Ghosh, 'The Bomb, the Budget and the Economy'.

20 Prakash Karat, 'BJP's Nuclear Gambit Leads to Surrender to U.S.', *People's Democracy*, November 22, 1998.

21 See *The Hindustan Times, The Hindu*, October 27, 1998.

22 Proceedings of the Rajya Sabha, December 15, 1998.

23 Prakash Karat, 'A lethal link', *Frontline*, June 19, 1998.

24 Proceedings of the Rajya Sabha, December 15, 1998.

25 *Suo motu* statement by Prime Minister Vajpayee in the Lok Sabha on May 27, 1998.

26 Prakash Karat, 'A lethal link'.

27 M.S. Golwalkar, 'Welcome Bigger War,' in chapter 25, part 1, *Bunch of Thoughts*, revised and enlarged edition, Sahitya Sindhu Prakashana, Bangalore, 1996, p. 326.

28 M.S. Golwalkar, 'Nation at War', chapter 25, part 2, ibid.

29 Press Conference of May 17, 1998.

30 *The National Agenda For Governance*, adopted by the BJP and twelve other coalition partners on March 18, 1998.

31 'Sanctions, a blessing in disguise, says RSS', *The Hindu*, May 15, 1998. The report quotes Sudarshan, speaking to the press at an RSS training camp in Hyderabad, as saying that 'the nuclear tests had enhanced the honour and prestige of the country and boosted the people's confidence'. Revealing that 'the Vajpayee government, during its earlier 13-day stint in office, proposed to go in for nuclear tests', Sudarshan put forward a conspiracy theory: 'But the information leaked and the American Government played its role in toppling the then BJP Government'.

32 *Organiser*, XLIX, 42, May 17, 1998. The cover legend reads, '25th year of Pokhran: Nuclear India'. A report on page 3 of the issue quotes K. Balu, Director of the Nuclear Waste Management Group at the Bhabha Atomic Research Centre in Trombay, as saying: 'Though . .

ancient Indian science had enough advanced knowledge on Nuclear Physics, it was the West that first used the knowledge for destructive purposes by dropping atom bombs on Hiroshima and Nagasaki to end the war they were losing'. According to the report, the senior BARC scientist added that 'what we did in Pokhran in 1974 was a small thing compared to what we are doing in this field now for peaceful purposes' but that if someone wanted a repeat of Pokhran, 'we can do it again'. Balu is quoted as qualifying all this with the remark, 'nobody is a winner in a nuclear war'.

33 Ibid., p. 3.

2 HORROR OF NUCLEAR WEAPONS

1 Introduction to 'Worldwide Nuclear Deployments 1998', accessible at the Natural Resources Defence Council web-site at www.nrdc.org/nrdc/nrdcpro/tkstock/download.html.

2 Ibid. The 1993 estimate is from 'Nuclear Notebook', *Bulletin of Atomic Scientists*, December 1993, p. 57, cited by Kalpana Chittaranjan in 'Five Decades of Nuclear Weapons' in *Nuclear India*, edited by Jasjit Singh, p. 66. The estimate of 36,000 is confirmed in Zia Mian and M.V. Ramana, 'Diplomatic Judo: Using the NPT to make the nuclear weapons states negotiate the abolition of nuclear weapons', a 10-page paper.

3 Zia Mian and M.V. Ramana, 'Diplomatic Judo'.

4 This assessment is by Jonathan Schell, *The Gift of Time: The Case For Abolishing Nuclear Weapons Now,* New York: Metropolitan Books, 1998; also available as a Penguin India book, 1998. In a review of the book, Michael Foot, the highly respected figure of the British Labour Left, refers to the Presidential directive as 'a real case for impeachment' of President Clinton; *Frontline*, December 4, 1998.

5 Introduction to 'Worldwide Nuclear Deployments 1998'.

6 Zia Mian and M.V. Ramana, 'Diplomatic Judo'.

7 'Practice what you preach, India tells Big Five at UN', *The Economic Times*, November 4, 1998 (online edition). The report quotes Dilip Lahiri, Additional Secretary, UN, External Affairs Ministry, speaking on a draft resolution moved by India calling for immediate steps to reduce the risk of unintentional and accidental use of nuclear weapons.

8 24 to 36 is the 'lower end figure' proposed by Jasjit Singh in *Nuclear India*, p. 315. 150 is the second-strike-capability-conferring figure proposed by General K. Sundarji in 1996. See C. Rammanohar Reddy, 'The wages of Armageddon-I', *The Hindu*.

9 The literature on Hiroshima and Nagasaki and on the effects of nuclear weapons is vast. The section below owes a great deal to two useful sources: N.D. Jayaprakash, *The Meaning of Hiroshima and Nagasaki*, Delhi Science Forum and Kerala Sastra Sahitya Parishad, 1990; and the *High Energy Weapons Archive* at http://www.fas.org/nuke/hew, especially the section, 'Nuclear Weapons: Frequently Asked Questions', by Carey Sublette.

10 From M.S. Swaminathan's speech at the Convention Against Nuclear Weapons, Chennai, July 26, 1998.

11 Rashid Naim, '*Aadhi Raat ke Baad* (After Midnight)', in *Nuclear Proliferation in South Asia*, edited by Stephen Cohen, Boulder: Westview Press, 1992; re-issued by the Program in Arms Control, Disarmament, and International Security, University of Illinois in June 1998, and accessible at the web-site, http://acdis.uluc.edu/.

12 M.V. Ramana, 'Bombing Bombay? Effects of Nuclear Weapons and a case study of a hypothetical nuclear explosion', a paper, p. 18.

13 The Head of the Bhabha Atomic Research Centre's Health, Safety, Environment Group suggested to the media, just before Pokhran-II, that India could survive a nuclear war. The prescriptions included taking iodine tablets, staying indoors, and consuming only stored food or powdered milk. People in the danger zone were advised to 'go to the ground floor, and if possible to the basement'. See *The Pioneer*, April 24, 1998. Arundhati Roy asks in 'The

End of Imagination': 'What do you do with these levels of lunacy? What do you do if you're trapped in an asylum and the doctors are all dangerously deranged?'

14 *The Hindu*, May 16, 1998.

15 Letter from Nagasaki by Mariko Kitano, accessible at the South Asians Against Nukes website, http://www.mnet.fr/aiindex/NoNukes.html.

16 *Atomic Audit: The Costs and Consequences of U.S. Nuclear Weapons Since 1940*, edited by Stephen I. Schwartz, Washington D.C.: Brookings Institution Press, 1998.

17 C. Rammanohar Reddy, 'Cost of Nuclear Weaponisation in India – Some Estimates', unpublished paper, 1998; see also 'The wages of Armageddon', *The Hindu*, August 31, September 1 and 2, 1998. All the figures that follow are from Reddy's estimates.

18 Jayati Ghosh, 'The Bomb, the Budget and the Economy', in *Out of Nuclear Darkness: The Indian Case For Disarmament*, MIND (Movement in India for Nuclear Disarmament), 1999.

3 DETTERENCE THEORY AND NUCLEAR THEOLOGY

1 Vajpayee spoke in Hindi on all three occasions. The first two quotes are from the official Indian translations of the speeches. The third has been unofficially translated.

2 Jonathan Schell, *The Abolition*, New York: Avon Books, 1986, pp. 51–54; Freeman J. Dyson, *Weapons and Hope*, Indian reprint, New Delhi: Allied Publishers, 1986, pp. 170–71.

3 The plan was named after Bernard Baruch, a financier who was an adviser to U.S. Presidents.

4 Dyson, *Weapons and Hope*, p. 171.

5 The minimum incurred cost of the U.S. nuclear weapons programme, 1940–1996, is estimated at $ 5.82 billion in *Atomic Audit: The Costs and Consequences of U.S. Nuclear Weapons since 1940*, edited by Stephen I. Schwartz, Washington D.C.: Brookings Institution, 1998.

6 In 1954, John Foster Dulles, hawkish Secretary of State in the Eisenhower administration, announced that any attack on the United States or its allies anywhere would be met 'in a manner and at a place of our own choosing'. The implication of this was referred to as 'massive retaliation'. See Kalpana Chittaranjan, 'Five Decades of Nuclear Weapons', in *Nuclear India*, edited by Jasjit Singh.

7 Henry Kissinger, *Nuclear Weapons and Foreign Policy*, New York: Harper & Brothers, 1957.

8 Dyson, *Weapons and Hope*, pp. 90–92.

9 Schell, *The Abolition*, pp. 60–62.

10 The term 'assured destruction' was first officially used by U.S. Defence Secretary Robert McNamara, who has come a long way since then.

11 Schell, *The Abolition*, pp. 73–74.

12 Kissinger, *Nuclear Weapons and Foreign Policy*, p. 132.

13 Schell, *The Gift of Time*, p. 47.

14 Ibid., pp. 181–208.

15 There is a substantial expert and scholarly literature on the subject. Two useful articles, written for lay readers and offering references to this literature, are 'Accidental Nuclear War' by Bruce G. Blair and Henry W. Kendall in *Scientific American*, December 1990, pp. 53–58; and 'Taking Nuclear Weapons off Hair-Trigger Alert', by Bruce G. Blair, Harold A. Feiveson and Frank N. von Hippel in *Scientific American*, November 1997, pp. 74–81.

16 Blair et. al., 'Taking Nuclear Weapons off Hair-Trigger Alert'.

17 *Indian Journal of International Law*, Volume 37, pp. 244–49.

18 The guru of the school of 'minimum credible nuclear deterrence' is K. Subrahmanyam. For representative versions of his views, see 'Arms Race Myth' and 'Not a Numbers Game' in *The Times of India* of May 30 and December 7, 1998. For the more extreme versions, see Brahma Chellaney, 'New Nuclear Clarity with Old Waffle' and 'Tactical Nukes', in *The Hindustan Times*, January 3 and January 27, 1999; and Bharat Karnad, 'A Thermonuclear

Deterrent', in *India's Nuclear Deterrent: Pokhran-II and Beyond*, edited by Amitabh Matoo, New Delhi: Har-Anand, 1999.

[19] See the contributions by Kalpana Chittaranjan and Manpreet Sethi in *Nuclear India*, edited by Jasjit Singh.

[20] Prime Minister Vajpayee replying in the Lok Sabha on March 15, 1999 to the debate on the motion of thanks to the President. Translated from the Hindi original.

[21] Bertrand Russell, *Common Sense and Nuclear Warfare*, London: Allen & Unwin, 1959. Russell, along with Joseph Rotblat, the distinguished British physicist who refused to continue work on the U.S. bomb, founded the Pugwash movement against nuclear weapons.

[22] Quoted by Michael Foot in *Dr Strangeglove, I Presume*, pp. 68–69.

[23] A.J.P. Taylor's *Romanes Lecture, 1988*, cited by Michael Foot, ibid., pp. 223–24.

4 SUBVERTING INDIA'S NUCLEAR POLICY

[1] *India Today*, May 25, 1998.

[2] See N. Ram, 'The Nuclear Dispute: An Indian Perspective', in *Conflicting Images: India and the United States* edited by Sulochana Raghavan Glazer and Nathan Glazer, Maryland: Glenn Dale, 1990, pp. 83–108.

[3] Constituent Assembly of India (Legislative) Debates, 2nd session, Volume 5 (1948), pp. 3319–33, cited by Itty Abraham in *The Making of the Indian Atomic Bomb: Science, Secrecy and the Postcolonial State*, New Delhi: Orient Longman, 1999. Abraham's book, despite its claims, appears to be a thinly argued, esoteric and pretentious attempt to ride some post-modernist hobby horses relating to discourses of national security and national development.

[4] For a 1980s discussion of the substance of this policy, see N. Ram, 'The Nuclear Dispute'.

[5] K. Subrahmanyam, 'Indian Nuclear Policy – 1964–98 (A personal recollection),' in *Nuclear India* edited by Jasjit Singh.

[6] Ibid., pp. 28–29.

[7] See N. Ram, 'The Nuclear Dispute', p. 97.

[8] As early as 1957 Bhabha spoke off the record to four British journalists about the desirability of India making nuclear weapons to 'deter China', even though China at that time had no nuclear weapons. Bhabha's view was completely at variance with those of Jawaharlal Nehru. The information comes from Sir John Maddox, Editor Emeritus, *Nature*, interviewed in Chennai on April 2, 1999. Maddox was one of the journalists present on that occasion as well as at a subsequent meeting two years later where Bhabha reiterated his views.

[9] See Robert S. Anderson, 'Building Scientific Institutions in India: Saha and Bhabha', Occasional Paper Series, No. 11, Center For Developing-Area Studies, McGill University, 1975, p. 81; also see Peter Pringle and James Spigelman, *The Nuclear Barons: The Inside Story of How They Created Our Nuclear Weapons*, London: Sphere Books, 1982.

[10] This is an assertion by K. Subrahmanyam in his reminiscential and undocumented 'Indian Nuclear Policy' in *Nuclear India*, p. 26.

[11] Ibid., pp. 26–27.

[12] For a useful bibliography, see *Pakistan and the Bomb: Public Opinion and Nuclear Options*, edited by Samina Ahmed and David Cortright, Indiana: University of Notre Dame Press, 1998.

5 SCIENCE, NUCLEAR CAPABILITIES AND THE BOMB

[1] Report in *The Hindu*, May 21, 1998.

[2] T.S. Subramanian, 'Fission power', *Frontline*, August 23, 1997; 'To full power', in *Frontline*, May 22, 1993.

[3] By 2000, India's nuclear power programme will have achieved less than a fifth of the original target set officially: 10,000 Mwe of installed nuclear power generating capacity by the

end of the century.

[4] Quoted in 'Safe science is the norm', by Kalpana Sharma, *The Hindu*, September 10, 1998. See also 'Why don't they speak out?' by Kalpana Sharma, *The Hindu*, September 9, 1998. These two articles mention some rare instances of senior Indian scientists taking a critical stance on the nuclear issue.

[5] Carey Sublette, 'Nuclear Weapons: Frequently Asked Questions'.

[6] Dyson, *Weapons and Hope*, p. 38.

[7] *The Hindu*, May16, 1998.

[8] 'Kashmir a separate issue', *The Hindu*, March 25, 1999.

[9] L. Ramdas, 'Pokhran-II and its fallout', *Frontline*, July 4, 1998; and V.R. Raghavan, 'India's nuclear dilemma', and 'Minimum nuclear deterrence', *The Hindu*, June 9, 1998 and September 8, 1998.

[10] *People's Democracy*, May 24, 1998.

[11] *The Deccan Herald*, March 4, 1998.

[12] On March 24, 1993, President F.W. de Klerk announced that six nuclear devices had been dismantled and destroyed before South Africa adhered to the NPT. For a critical discussion of the policy, see Ruchita Beri, 'South Africa's Nuclear Policy', in *Strategic Analysis*, XXII, 7, October 1998.

[13] For an excellent interpretative political history, see Avner Cohen, *Israel And The Bomb*, New York: Columbia University Press, 1998.

[14] 'Weaponization now complete, say scientists', *The Hindu*, May 18, 1998. See also Joint Statement by DAE and DRDO, May 17, 1998.

[15] *Frontline*, May 26, 1998.

[16] *New York Times* report by James F. Burns, reproduced in *The Times of India*, May 26, 1998.

[17] The material in this section is based primarily on the published work of Richard Garwin (and co-authors), a U.S. nuclear weapons expert and a specialist on the scientific aspects of CTBT-related questions; and Carey Sublette's 'Nuclear Weapons: Frequently Asked Questions'. See especially 'Nuclear weapon development without nuclear testing' by R. Garwin and Vadim A. Simonenko, paper prepared for the Pugwash Workshop on 'Problems in Achieving a Nuclear Weapon-Free World', October 1996; 'The Maintenance of Nuclear Weapon Stockpiles Without Nuclear Explosion Testing' by R. Garwin, paper submitted to the 24th Pugwash Workshop on Nuclear Forces, September 1996; and 'The Future of Nuclear Weapons Without Nuclear Testing' by R. Garwin in *Arms Control Today*, 27, 8, November/December 1997. All the Garwin papers are available at the Nuclear Resources section of the Federation of American Scientists web-site at http://www.fas.org. We have also used 'The Role of Nuclear Tests in Nuclear Weapon Design: Some Technical Aspects' by Tushar Ravuri, from the Union of Concerned Scientists web-site at http://www.ucsusa.org.

[18] Joint Statement by DAE and DRDO, May 17, 1998.

[19] S.K. Sikka and Anil Kakodkar, 'Some Preliminary Results of May 11-13, 1998 Nuclear Detonations at Pokhran', BARC newsletter, May/June 1998.

[20] *India Today*, October 12, 1998.

[21] Buddhi Kota Subba Rao, 'The H-bomb issue is crucial', *Frontline*, June 19, 1998.

[22] For a brief summary of the issues involved, see T. Jayaraman, 'Yields called into question', *Frontline*, October 23, 1998.

[23] A. Gopalakrishnan, 'How credible is our deterrence?', *The Hindu*, November 18, 1998; and 'Margins of error, Verifying claims on nuclear tests', *The Times of India*, November 20, 1998.

[24] A Special Correspondent, 'Matters of technology', *Frontline*, July 17, 1998.

[25] 'India's Economic Diplomacy in the post-Pokhran Era', transcript of a seminar held on September 12, 1998 published by the Rajiv Gandhi Institute for Contemporary Studies in November 1998.

26 Joint Statement by the DAE and DRDO, May 17, 1998.

27 Interview, *The Hindustan Times*, September 22, 1998.

28 P.K. Iyengar, 'Just Say No', *India Today*, November 9, 1998; A. Gopalakrishnan, 'How credible is our deterrence?', *The Hindu*, November 18, 1998; and Brahma Chellaney, 'India's Trial by Atom', *The Hindustan Times*, November 4, 1998. Subsequently, Chellaney has defended the claim of thermonuclear capability; 'India's hydrogen bomb', *The Hindustan Times*, January 13, 1999.

29 Interview, *Frontline*, January 15, 1999.

30 Dinesh Kumar, 'IAF still lacks N-capability', *The Times of India*, October 18, 1998.

6 NUCLEAR WEAPONS AND SECURITY IN SOUTH ASIA

1 Prime Minister's Statement, Rajya Sabha, December 15, 1998.

2 'When that bomb went off in 1974, I was in New Delhi serving as our Ambassador. I recall saying to the Foreign Secretary and to the Prime Minister: "You have done something disastrous. You have absolute hegemony in South Asia today, and yet you set off this bomb. The day will come in ten years' time when there will be a Mogul general in power in Islamabad and he will call you one day and say, 'I have four bombs, one for Madras, one for Calcutta, one for Bombay and one for Delhi. We would like the Punjab and Kashmir back by Thursday, or we'll all meet in heaven on Friday". . . . That is geopolitics for you.' See *The Hindu*, November 24, 1981.

3 See Swaran Singh, 'China's Nuclear Weapons and Doctrine', in *Nuclear India*, edited by Jasjit Singh. His basic argument is that no first-use does not bar the Chinese from 'nuking' what they consider to be their own territory, such as the Aksai Chin, and hence India cannot trust China's no first-use posture.

4 Proceedings of the Rajya Sabha, December 15, 1998.

5 'Pakistan should respond, says COAS', *Dawn*, April 13, 1999.

6 'Agni-II successfully test-fired', *The Hindu*, April 12, 1999.

7 'Is Accidental Nuclear War Impossible?', *The Asian Age*, December 16, 1998.

8 For the texts, see *The Hindu* and other Indian newspapers of February 22, 1999.

9 'N-arms deployment a reciprocal matter', *The Hindu*, November 11, 1998.

10 'U.S. must persuade India, says Pak.', *The Hindu*, December 13, 1998.

7 WHY NOT JOIN THE CTBT AND THE FMCT?

1 On May 14, 1998, the day after the Vajpayee government conducted the second round of tests at Pokhran, K.S. Sudarshan, the joint general secretary of the RSS, publicly welcomed the U.S. economic sanctions as a 'blessing in disguise'. He asserted that the nuclear tests had enhanced the 'honour' and 'prestige' of the country. 'Sanctions, a blessing in disguise, says RSS', *The Hindu*, May 15, 1998.

2 Praful Bidwai and Achin Vanaik, 'Why India Should Sign the CTBT: Returning to Our Own Agenda', *Economic and Political Weekly*, September 19, 1998.

3 'CTBT: Can India resist this blackmail?', *The Hindu*, July 12, 1996.

4 'CTBT: playing the end-game', *The Hindu*, June 13, 1996.

5 Press conference by Ambassador Prakash Shah, UN Secretariat document, August 30, 1996. All subsequent quotes attributed to Ambassador Shah are from this document.

6 'India will not sign CTBT unconditionally: PM', *The Hindu*, May 15, 1998. Three days earlier, Brajesh Mishra, Principal Secretary to the Prime Minister, had announced in a written statement that India was ready to become an 'adherent to some of the undertakings of the CTBT', but its position on the treaty would not be determined in a 'vacuum': 'It would necessarily be an evolutionary process from concept to commitment and would depend on a number of reciprocal activities'. See *The Hindu*, May 12, 1998. This high ground was

subsequently given up under U.S. and western pressure.

7 Joint Communiqué on Indian and Pakistan Nuclear Tests by the Foreign Ministers of the Five Permanent Members of the Security Council, press release dated June 5, 1998; UN Security Council Resolution 1172, adopted unanimously on June 6, 1998; G-8 Foreign Ministers Communiqué on Indian and Pakistan Nuclear Tests, issued at Lancaster House, London, June 12, 1998.

8 On November 9, President Clinton issued a notification easing some sanctions against Pakistan and India, but the bias towards Pakistan, reflected in the decision to support Pakistan's bid for an aid package from the International Monetary Fund (IMF), was widely criticized in the Indian press. See, for example, K.K. Katyal, 'India not impressed by U.S. arguments on sanctions', *The Hindu*, November 12, 1998.

9 See *The Hindu* and other Indian daily newspapers of November 14, 1998 for a full list of the targeted 'entities', scientific research institutions and public and private sector organizations having even the remotest connection or dealings with the Departments of Atomic Energy and Space and the Defence Research and Development Organization.

10 Strobe Talbott, 'U.S. Diplomacy in South Asia: A Progress Report', Federal News Service, Washington D.C.

11 *The Times of India*, November 13, 1998.

12 'India, Pakistan will sign CTBT', *The Hindu*, February 11, 1999. Albright was speaking at the Wesleyan University, Middletown, Connecticut.

13 'CTBT: playing the end-game', *The Hindu*, June 13, 1996.

14 'CTBT and nuclear hegemony', *The Hindu*, January 18, 1996.

15 Statement accessible on http://www.peacenet.org/disarm/ctbt.html.

16 Press conference at the United Nations, New York, UN Secretariat document, September 12, 1996.

17 Statement in Lok Sabha, May 27, 1998.

18 IDSA home page, http://www.idsa-india.org.

19 Savita Dutt, 'Fissile Material Cut-Off Treaty: A Critique', *Strategic Analysis*, XXI, 18, February 1998, pp. 1685–1701. 'Judging from the way India has reacted to the CTBT', she observes, 'it has become quite obvious that a Fissile Material Ban (in its present form) like the CTBT is also considered to be not in the national interest of the country. By no stretch of the imagination can it be considered a non-discriminatory disarmament measure.'

20 Praful Bidwai, 'An unequal deal', *Frontline*, September 11, 1998.

8 GETTING OFF THE TIGER: AN AGENDA FOR DEWEAPONIZATION

1 The voluntary moratorium became an implied and then an explicit part of official Indian nuclear policy after the second round of nuclear explosions on May 13, 1998. In his Statement of May 27 in Parliament Prime Minister Vajpayee noted, 'Subsequently, Government has already announced that India will now observe a voluntary moratorium and refrain from conducting underground nuclear test explosions', adding: 'We have also indicated willingness to move towards a *de jure* formalization of this declaration'. The voluntary moratorium on testing has figured in most official explications of India's nuclear policy in recent months.

2 See Statement of International Atomic Energy Agency (IAEA) Director General Hans Blix to the Board of Governors on South Africa's nuclear weapons programme, March 31,1993, IAEA document; also Blix's Statement to the Forty-eighth session of the United Nations General Assembly, New York, November 1, 1993, IAEA document. For a critical discussion of the policy, see Ruchita Beri, 'South Africa's Nuclear Policy', in *Strategic Analysis*, XXII, 7, October 1998.

GLOSSARY

atomic number: A number characteristic of every element that denotes the number of protons (particles with a positive unit charge) in the nucleus of the atom.
atomic weight: A number denoting the total number of protons and neutrons in the nucleus of every atom. Atoms of a given element may have different atomic weights (called isotopes) due to variations in the number of neutrons in the nucleus.
C^3I: Command, control, communications and intelligence. This refers to the entire complex of activities required to control the use and authorization to use of nuclear weapons, including all the associated tasks. It also includes the activity associated with being on the alert and watching for signals of a possible nuclear attack.
computer simulation: Reproducing on the computer a process or the behaviour of a device, by modelling the process or the behaviour using mathematical methods. In the particular case of nuclear weapons, the term refers to studying the behaviour of a nuclear weapon or its components under different conditions by similar means.
counter-force strategy: The concept in deterrence theory of targeting primarily the military assets of the opposite side. Although made much of in deterrence theory, it appears that this is what armies always do; they always prefer targetting the military assets of the enemy.
critical mass: The minimum amount of fissile material necessary for a self-sustaining chain reaction to develop. The amount depends on the density and shape of the material.
deuterium: An isotope of the element hydrogen. This has one proton and one neutron in its nucleus. When deuterium is present instead of hydrogen (that has only one proton and no neutrons) in water molecules, the liquid is known as heavy water.
deployment: Referring to the situation when a particular armament is available with the armed forces in ready-to-use condition. In the case of nuclear weapons, it refers

to weapons that are fitted to delivery systems and are ready to be used.

electromagnetic radiation: All radiation, from heat to radio waves to X-rays and gamma rays, is basically the same. These rays are travelling electric and magnetic waves. Referred to by the comprehensive term. electromagnetic radiation, all these variants differ only in their frequencies. The physical effects they cause depend on the frequencies.

equation-of-state: An expression that describes how quantities like pressure, volume, temperature, etc. are related to each other for a given substance.

fast-breeder reactor: A type of nuclear power reactor that produces more of the fissile material, plutonium (Pu-239), than it consumes. It uses plutonium (Pu-239) and depleted uranium (predominantly U-238) as fuel and, in the process, produces more plutonium than put in initially.

fission: The process by which the nucleus of an atom splits into two or more pieces. It may be spontaneous or induced (typically by a neutron striking the nucleus). Fissile materials used in weapons or reactors are those that undergo induced fission.

flexible response: Another piece of jargon from deterrence theory referring to the ability to respond with nuclear weapons to any attack in a graduated manner, typically without immediately launching Intercontinental Ballistic Missiles (ICBMs).

fusion: The process whereby two nuclei come together to form a third composite nucleus. Of relevance to the discussion in the text are different means of fusion of the isotopes of hydrogen. Some six possible means exist, including the fusion of two deuterium nuclei as well as the fusion of a deuterium nucleus and a tritium nucleus.

ground zero: The point on the ground directly below an exploding nuclear weapon.

high-alert status: The state in which the delivery systems, mainly missiles, of nuclear warheads are kept by the United States and Russia. In particular, this implies that these missiles can be launched within a few minutes after the order to launch them is issued. The order to launch can be decided and conveyed to the operational units that actually fire the missiles within minutes.

highly enriched uranium: This is material obtained by processing natural uranium so that the isotope of atomic weight 235 (referred to often as U-235, U indicating uranium) is present in much larger quantities, typically of the order of 20% of the total, than in natural uranium. Weapons-grade highly enriched uranium can have a much higher percentage of U-235, typically up to about 80 per cent.

hydrotests: Tests where the properties of fissile material are studied, including those in a weapons configuration, but with the actual fissile material replaced by inert material. The term 'hydro' appears because in the range of conditions for which the properties of the fissile material are studied, the material behaviour is similar to that of a fluid.

hydrodynamic codes: Computer programmes that incorporate the equations that govern the behaviour of fluids and are relevant to the description of the behaviour of the fissile material in nuclear weapons.

hydronuclear tests: These are tests of nuclear weapons where actual fission energy is released and the yield is non-zero. It is not easy to control these tests, which tend to give yields much larger than expected. Such tests cannot be conducted by signatories to the CTBT.

isotopes: Atoms of the same element that have different atomic weights. Isotopes have the same chemical properties but may differ in their physical properties.

induction: Refers to the provision of armaments to the armed forces for use. In the context of nuclear weapons, the term is used to refer to the provision of nuclear warheads for use by the armed forces.
kiloton: One thousand tonnes.
limited nuclear war: Yet another myth of deterrence theory. This term describes the idea that a nuclear confrontation may either be confined to a geographically definite region or involve the use of only a part of the nuclear arsenals of the opposing forces, or both. However, serious analysis of the implications of limited nuclear war seem to have always resulted in the conclusion that it would eventually involve the entire nuclear arsenal of both sides. Since no nuclear war of this nature has been fought (mercifully, of course), there is no way of deterring the promoters of this idea from talking about it.
megaton: One million tonnes.
nuclear weapons codes: A general term covering the full suite of computer programmes that describe the behaviour of nuclear weapons during the initiation and development of the explosion.
neutronic codes: Computer programmes that describe the behaviour of the neutrons in the fissile material of the nuclear weapon during the process of explosion.
one-dimensional and two-dimensional codes: In the context in which it appears here, it refers to those nuclear weapons codes that specifically use the symmetry of the weapon design (spherical or cylindrical symmetry) to simplify the calculations. The symmetry ensures that the number of physical dimensions effectively involved in the calculations is reduced to one or two, instead of the usual three.
radiation: In the context of Chapter 2, it refers to all emissions from radioactive substances. The emissions include particles as well as electromagnetic radiation. The use in this sense of the term, radiation, is distinguished by the context from its use as scientific shorthand for elecromagnetic radiation.
seismology: The branch of the discipline of geology that studies earthquakes. However, significant effort has also been spent in studying the signals, similar to earthquake signals, that come from man-made explosions, particularly nuclear explosions. Such explosions also produce waves that travel through the earth.
tactical nuclear weapons: These are nuclear weapons relatively small in size and yield that are meant for use as artillery shells and in very short-range missiles.
tritium: An isotope of hydrogen that has one proton and two neutrons in the nucleus.
weapons-grade plutonium: Plutonium has a number of isotopes. When plutonium is processed to ensure that the isotope of atomic weight 239 (Pu-239, where Pu indicates plutonium) is predominant, it is referred to as weapons-grade plutonium. The principal contaminant is the plutonium isotope of atomic weight 240 (Pu-240); weapons-grade plutonium has usually less than 7 per cent of this contaminant.
yield: In the context of nuclear weapons, this term refers to the explosive power of the nuclear weapon or explosive. It is measured in units of the number of tons of TNT (a chemical explosive) that would produce an explosion of equivalent intensity.
yield-to-weight ratio: A number that is of significance in designing nuclear weapons. Since delivery systems like missiles or aircraft have an upper limit on the weight they can carry (referred to as payload capacity), the weapons designer has to ensure that the design produces as powerful an explosion as possible while minimizing the weight of the weapon.